C000184177

RAMBLES
AROUND MANCHESTER
– walks within 25 miles
of the city centre

MIKE CRESSWELL
Photographs by Reg Timms

SIGMA LEISURE

Wilmslow, England

AMAZING!

I keep being amazed! And I'm amazed that I keep being amazed because I should know better.

I sat down to list some of my favourite walks and was amazed to find how many of them were within 25 miles of the middle of Manchester, which is probably not many people's idea of a scenic centre. I was amazed to find just how many marvellous walks start within 25 miles, as the crow flies, of the heart of the great city, how many superb walking areas are within that distance: the dramatic South Pennines around Hebden Bridge, the gritty hills of the Dark Peak and the lighter charms of the White Peak, Cheshire's Delamere Forest and Sandstone Trail, the hills and plain of West Lancashire, the rich greenness of the Ribble valley.

My amazement was unabated when I thought about the contrasts in landscape such as the flat mosslands around Martin Mere, the thrilling escarpments of sandstone at Frodsham and gritstone at Kinder Scout, the limestone gorge of Cheedale. There are the Pennine valleys, narrow and deep-cut in Calderdale, even gouged right through England's backbone by glacial meltwater at Summit, or the green vales of Edale and Hope, and high ridges and plateaux and isolated hills in plenty. There are forest and moorland and rolling green pastures – and extensive views across man-made metropolitan Manchester from the hills around it.

I was amazed at the extremes of weather to be found, fighting my way through thigh-deep snow to reach Stoodley Pike or scuttling from tree to tree along the towpath of the Peak Forest Canal to seek shade with the temperature in the 90s, or seeing the waterfall at Kinder Downfall blown back high into the air by a gale-force wind.

Amazing too are the buildings to be seen: great houses such as Stonyhurst and Lyme, more humble ones such as the almshouses and church at Stydd, and so many cottages and their gardens. And what about fantastic Little Moreton Hall and the nearby folly tower on Mow Cop? And the Roman fort at Castleshaw and the possible Roman road on Blackstone Edge and canals and railway tunnels and . . . ? Amazing!

And all on walks beginning within 25 miles of the middle of Manchester. So, if you live anywhere in or near Greater Manchester, these walks are amazingly easy to reach by car or public transport. A few of them are well-known walks in all or part, but I've tried to include many that aren't. I'd be amazed if anyone has walked all these routes.

There are sixteen chapters, each describing a main walk – one $8^1/_2$ miles, one of 18 miles, and the rest between 10 and 13 miles in length. But there are lots of shorter – and some longer – variations to produce about 100 walks in total, from 3 miles to $19^1/_2$, so I'd be amazed if there isn't plenty to suit you.

With the advice in the Feetnotes, the information at the beginning of each chapter and the detailed descriptions of the walks, my amazement would be great if you couldn't find your way, and my amazement would increase if you didn't enjoy yourself in exploring this amazing area which is so good for walking.

I said I was amazed but should have known better. That's because I have been experiencing and appreciating these walks for so long that I had never sat down and worked out just how close to Manchester they all were. I'd like to think that people will come from farther afield to stay in the area so that their amazement can be added to that of those who live here.

Yes, come and be delighted by this amazing area, full of beauty and interest and wonderful walking, aided, of course, by the amazed author and his amazing book!

Mike Cresswell

CONTENTS

FEETNOTES

1. You will see from the location map that the walks are well spread with Manchester at their heart, but, not least because there are so many walks I could have included, two excellent walking areas are excluded, the Cheshire Peak District and the West Pennines. For walks in those two areas, I urge you to look to two other books from Sigma Leisure: Graham Beech's "East Cheshire Walks: from Peak to Plain" and my own "West Pennine Walks".

2. The main walk in each chapter is circular and each chapter contains a variation or variations producing shorter or longer walks, sometimes circular and sometimes linear. All the main walks and most of the variations are accessible by public transport – which is what I used for all these walks. But, fear not, I do provide instructions on how to reach the starting-points by car, too. The travel directions are given as though you were coming from Manchester although I appreciate many of you won't be, but it would be too difficult to cater for all possible places of origin. You shouldn't have any difficulty in finding the starting-points but, if you do, I'm not sure that you can be trusted to find your way round the walks, either!

3. At the beginning of each chapter, I refer to the relevant Ordnance Survey maps needed for the walk, because, although I hope you find the combination of text and sketch-map will lead you safely round the walk, I do recommend carrying maps as well. They make a walk more interesting if you can identify all the features around, you might stray off the route, or you might wish to cut the walk short if the weather turns bad – or *you* do! I have given details of the relevant Pathfinder 1:25000 maps and Landranger 1:50000 maps, except for those walks covered by the Outdoor Leisure 1:25000 maps, which are such good value that it's worth buying them in preference to either of the other series.

4. In the course of the walk descriptions, which begin with the main walk and then set out the variations, I try to avoid giving precise distances between features, or compass bearings or references to compass points, and I avoid timings completely, as I find all these confuse less experienced walkers, who are so busy worrying about them that they miss the relevant instructions in the text. So, I include such

details only where I think they will be of particular assistance – and I assume experienced walkers will be able to look after themselves.

5. At the time of writing, there is a train or bus at least hourly on Mondays to Saturdays to the start (and finish) of all the main walks except 5 and 12, where it's approximately 2-hourly, but services are likely to be less frequent or even non-existent on Sundays. At least hourly access to the walks was my intention except in the case of the Wyedale walk (Walk 12) which amply justifies a little inconvenience, but unfortunately the service to Ribchester (Walk 5) was reduced when the book was almost complete.

I have not given precise details of bus services because, since deregulation, they can change often and with little warning, and even train services alter more frequently than they used to. So, if you are intending to use public transport, it is worth telephoning the appropriate enquiry line before you are marooned out in the wilds somewhere, assuming you even reach the start of the walk. Greater Manchester Enquiry Line (061 228 7811) will provide most of the bus and train information you need but also of assistance will be: West Yorkshire Enquiry Line (0532 457676) for buses around Hebden Bridge on Walk 1 and to return to Todmorden on Walk 2; Lancashire Enquiry Line (0772 263333) for buses beyond Blackburn on Walks 4 and 5 and from Martin Mere to Burscough Bridge on Walk 6; and Cheshire Enquiry Line (0244 602666) for the Frodsham/Kingsley/Hatchmere bus on Walk 8.

It's worth ascertaining whether a Wayfarer ticket, which you can use on buses and trains, or a day ticket from one of the bus companies will reduce the cost of travel for all or part of any of these walks. I've made great use of the Wayfarer in the preparation of this book.

6. Finally, my thanks to Reg Timms for the excellent fruits of his photographic excursions along the routes of these walks; to the Editor of the "Bolton Evening News" for allowing me to base some of these walks on my articles "Mike's Hikes" which have appeared in the paper (although all have been rewalked, and updated where necessary); to all those who have enlivened these walks by a friendly chat when I have encountered them (and there has been no occasion when I have been faced with an unfriendly chat); and to my wife, Chris, for her company on some of the walks and her support and encouragement on all of them.

LOCATION MAP

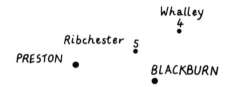

Whalley
4
•

Ribchester 5
•

PRESTON
•

BLACKBURN
•

SOUTHPORT
•

                                                                    BURY
Burscough Bridge 6   7 Parbold   •
                  •   •
                              WIGAN   BOLTON
                              •   •

                                       MANCHESTER◉

LIVERPOOL   WARRINGTON
•   •

        8 Frodsham
        •

CHESTER
•

BRADFORD
•
•LEEDS

! Hebden Bridge
•

2
•
Todmorden   •
HALIFAX

3 Littleborough   • HUDDERSFIELD
•

•ROCHDALE   16 Marsden
•

15 Uppermill
•

•
OLDHAM

STOCKPORT   SHEFFIELD
•   •
        10
Marple • 14 Hayfield   13 Hope
        •   •

        11 Whaley Bridge
        •

        BUXTON   12 Wyedale
        •   •
•
MACCLESFIELD

9 Congleton
•

N
⇑

STOKE-ON-TRENT
•

1. BEECHES AND BOULDERS

Hebden Bridge – Midge Hole – Lumb Hole – Hardcastle Crags – Hebble Hole – Heptonstall – Hebden Bridge.

Distance: between 3 miles and 12 miles.

Starting points:

Hebden Bridge railway station; Outdoor Leisure Map 21, South Pennines, map reference 395268.

Midge Hole; Outdoor Leisure Map 21, South Pennines, map reference 388292.

How to get there:

By car – to Hebden Bridge on the A646 between Todmorden and Halifax. Hebden Bridge railway station, with car park, is on the right-hand side of the A646 just beyond the town centre.

– for Midge Hole, turn left along the A6033 (for Keighley) in Hebden Bridge and, after about $1/2$ mile, bear left, signposted to Hardcastle Crags. At Midge Hole, at the end of the road, are car parks.

By train – to Hebden Bridge on the Manchester to Halifax line.

By bus – there is a bus service between Hebden Bridge and Midge Hole.

If that marvellous area, near Hebden Bridge, known as Hardcastle Crags has a defect, it is its justifiable popularity. If you want to be alone, don't go on a sunny, summer weekend, for multitudes know what a wonderful place it is for walking. But do make sure you go sometime as it's too good to miss.

This is a land of deep, narrow, well-wooded and well-watered valleys, with open hilltops between. The main walk, of 12 miles if you start at Hebden Bridge or 10 if you start at Midge Hole, samples three of these valleys – Crimsworth Dean, Hebden Dale and Colden Valley – the gorgeous spots of Lumb Hole and Hebble Hole, and fabulous, fantastic, hilltop Heptonstall.

There is so much to experience and enjoy on these walks that I am in danger of making this introduction far too long. Quite apart from these valleys and hills, Hebden Bridge and Heptonstall deserve half a day each, and I thoroughly recommend the "Hebden Bridge Trail" and "Heptonstall Trail" guidebooks published by the Calder Civic Trust and available in both places.

I had better just say that I provide a number of variations and you could easily split the walk in two and see even more of Hebden Dale with walks of $10^1/_2$ miles from Hebden Bridge via Midge Hole, Lumb Hole, Gibson Mill, Midge Hole and back to Hebden Bridge and 8 miles from Hebden Bridge to Midge Hole, Gibson Mill and Heptonstall and back to Hebden Bridge. From Midge Hole those walks would be $7^1/_2$ and $5^1/_2$ miles respectively. Or Hebden Bridge to Gibson Mill by an easy route and returning by an energetic one would be $6^1/_2$ miles, or a similar walk from Midge Hole would be only 3 miles.

Is that confusing? Well, the map should help, but, best of all of course, go out and try some of the walks – and see what happens.

The Walk

From Hebden Bridge railway station, take the drive down to the left, across the River Calder and the Rochdale Canal to the main road. Turn left along the road and then up the first road on the right (the A6033) to Keighley, Commercial Street. Just before you turn, look at the left-hand end of the house on the right with the nameplate "Machpelah". Consult your concordance (which you no doubt have with you) for the biblical origin of the name and then look at the two rows of windows, of 14 and 15 lights, which illuminated a fustian-cutting workshop.

Keep going, along the main road with the town centre down to your left and the whole town both up and down to right and left. Follow the sign for Hardcastle Crags and then, opposite the Nutclough House Hotel, turn down Foster Lane to leave the Keighley road, and fork left to continue downhill below double-decker dwellings and past interesting two-storey ones. Finally you pass new stone houses to arrive at an old stone packhorse bridge over the Hebden Water.

Across the bridge, turn right through the wall for the riverside path to

Walk 1

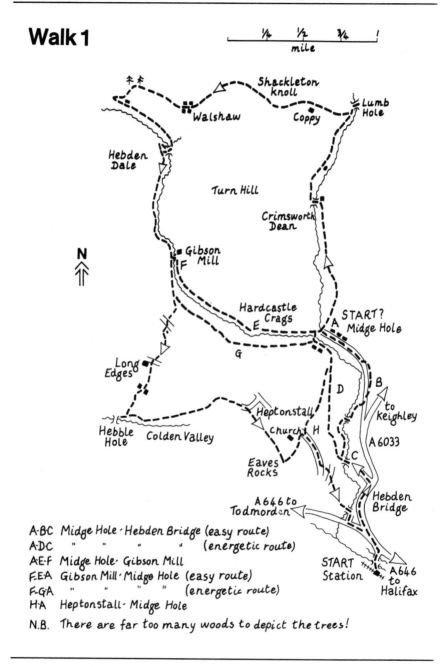

A·B·C Midge Hole · Hebden Bridge (easy route)
A·D·C   "   "   "   "   (energetic route)
A·E·F Midge Hole · Gibson Mill
F·E·A Gibson Mill · Midge Hole (easy route)
F·G·A   "   "   "   "   (energetic route)
H·A Heptonstall · Midge Hole

N.B. There are far too many woods to depict the trees!

Hardcastle Crags. A heron rose from the river, settled in a tree, and decided we were to be avoided and so took to a tree up the hillside. There were pied wagtails on the cricket pitch and dippers on stones in the river.

Cross the footbridge by the bowling green and follow the path between the Hebden Water and the old leat and then over the leat beside its weir. Cross the road, climb the steps, and turn left along the track, which curves round the hillside. Ahead is the Stoodley Pike-like Pecket Monument above Midge Hole.

When you reach the road, cross it and climb the steps opposite into Spring Wood. The path keeps you off the streets – and through the bluebells. You have to join the road at the approach to Midge Hole.

If you have walked from Hebden Bridge, turn right along the path immediately before the public conveniences. If coming from either of the car parks, walk back towards Hebden Bridge and turn left immediately after the public conveniences. You are now on the route of the Calderdale Way for a few yards. Do not go through the metal gate on the left but continue up the old bridleway leading to Pecket Well as far as the wooden wicket-gate on the left, with footpath sign, on the outside of the bend.

Now head up the rocky field by a sunken path, across a pair of ruts, and again up the sunken path to a gap in the wall, with a waymark post. Keep uphill to the next waymark and from there bear right even more uphill to the gate in the corner of the field. There is a fine view back to the trees above Midge Hole.

Now follow the level path through Middle Dean Wood, a hillside of beeches and boulders. Do not be tempted up to the right by the more obvious path but maintain the same level, passing a waymark. That points your way down towards the wall and you then follow the wall ahead to its corner and on to the next waymark. The path is clear above the reservoirs and then keeps some way up the hillside with a leat and Crimsworth Dean Beck below.

Through a gate you emerge into the open, upper valley of Crimsworth Dean. Follow the path along the hillside, through the next gate, over the stile, and so to another gate with a sweet little arch in the wall to the right. Turn left on the far side of the gate to keep between fence and hedge past a handsome house. The stone-slabbed path leads between ducks and over a stone bridge.

Now climb the steep path ahead between tall pines, a good place for red squirrels, I suspect. Across the stile, keep on up to the corner of the wood and then turn right along the track towards the farm. There's a good view back down the valley.

Obey the waymark to keep above the buildings and the wall and over the step-stile with its magnificent "thruff-stane". The grassy path leads you along the valley side, through the bracken, and there is a view back to Stoodley Pike. The path joins a track and you descend to delectable Lumb Hole, with its two waterfalls – one tall and slim and the other short and wide – and slender packhorse bridge.

" . . . two waterfalls . . . and slender packhorse bridge" – Lumb Hole

It's a good spot for a sheltered lunch; we sat under the big larch between the two cascades and took our fill of the delicious sights and sounds, and pasties and apple slices and . . .

Return up the track down which you came. Now continue up the walled track, with Crimsworth Dean, Heptonstall church and Stoodley Pike a marvellous sight to your left. When you reach the ruined buildings, turn up to the right beside the wall and climb to the gateway on the skyline to the left of the next ruin.

Turn right through the gateway and then left, through the gate and up the walled track towards Shackleton Knoll. You pass the ruin of Coppy and the hilltop landscape has a very different feel from that in the valley.

Through the next gateway, you follow the path by the left-hand wall. Now there are wonderfully-wide views over the South Pennines and down into Hebden Bridge. As the path swings round to the right, reservoirs come into view and the upper reaches of the valley of the Hebden Water are below them.

At the large sign, go through the wicket-gate on the left and along by the wall on the right. A curlew called, and another and another. The wall-side path takes you easily and comfortably down to a gate and, through it, you follow the track ahead with, to the right, the farm with the memorable name of Horodiddle. I wonder what its derivation is.

The track keeps to the right of a barn with a curvaceous roof and there are views of Stoodley Pike over the trees of the Hebden Water valley. The track acquires walls and takes you through the farmyard at Walshaw, between the houses and along the hillside, with Hebden Dale down to the left and looking interesting.

A few minutes' walk along the drive brings you to a wood and opposite is a stile over which you go. Bear right to a step-stile with a white waymark before a higher length of wall. Beware the steps on the far side! Make for the white-painted gateposts down to the left and go through the gate, with the valley impressive at your feet. Descend to the right and through a wall among heather and bilberries to reach a walled path, along which you turn left. Now mind your head on the oak tree.

Keep to the right of the attractive house. I assume that is a comfortable and commodious pigsty to the right of the path, and are those carvings at the end of the house portraits of former residents of the pigsty?

Follow the track past the house and just beyond it a beautiful stream gallops down the rocky hillside. Keep on along the main track through the trees until, just after crossing a stream, the track starts to rise. There take the path to the right down to a footbridge over the Hebden Water.

On the far bank you may be able to follow the riverside path to the left, but it was closed the last time I was there. You then have a choice. You can either turn right for a few paces and then climb very steeply up the hillside to a flight of steps which will take you onto the track at the top, where you turn left. Or you can follow the track rather more gently up to the right and eventually back to the left to the top of the steps up which others may have toiled.

Then all keep along the track with the farmhouse at Walshaw across the valley to your left and Shackleton Knoll to its right. The track descends gently and eventually returns you to the river. Again keep on downstream, fording side-streams on rocks among tree-roots.

The narrow, rocky path along the bank brings you to a reservoir. The path beside it then takes you past Gibson Mill (on the opposite bank), an early-19th century mill which I always feel would make an excellent Youth Hostel only half a mile from the Pennine Way. Here you need to decide whether to return directly to Midge Hole or Hebden Bridge or to start the second part of the walk via Heptonstall.

For Heptonstall, do not cross the bridge but continue up the rising track ahead, which gives a good view down into the valley of Hebden Dale, soon to be left behind. A yaffle laughed when I was last here because it knew that, where the track turns back to the right, we were about to ascend the long flight of steps ahead, as you must to reach Heptonstall. It's a quick and easy (!) way up the valley side. If you think climbing them is an achievement, what about constructing them?

When you cross a stream, you are almost at the top and can look with satisfaction down into the valley and onto Gibson Mill.

Go through the wicket-gate out of the wood and into the field with houses suddenly close. Ascend first beside the wall on the left and then that on the right and out onto the road. Turn left along the road and you can look down on the Pecket Monument and into Midge Hole, and back to your left are the farm buildings at Walshaw.

Turn up the walled drive to the first house on the right, Acre Lane Cottage, left beyond the house, and up the curving, walled path.

When the walls spread out, climb up to the benches and turn left, with Heptonstall and its church now down to your left. Behind you, beyond the fascinating pattern of walls on Turn Hill, Shackleton Knoll has now appeared, and Stoodley Pike comes into view ahead. Away to the left Emley Moor television mast was visible, too, when I last did this walk.

Cross the track ahead and follow your track as it curves round the wall on the right and down to the road beside sheds. Take a dozen paces to the right along the road and then turn left before the row of stone houses at Long Edges.

Go down the farm drive, through the gateway, and, still on the drive, bear right along the right-hand wall, down to the farm buildings. Ascend the step on the right between the modern building and the old one and through the legs of the telegraph pole. The next stile leads across the field to another one, and beyond that you turn down by the wall on the left. Look at the row of weavers' houses now behind you. The path is on an old stone causey, with Heptonstall church still to the left.

Near the bottom of the field bear right to the gap in the wall at the foot of the field. Bear right again between the stone posts, and again down by the left-hand wall and across to the right to a stile. Now descend to the right on the stone path beyond.

When the path turns more steeply downhill, you join the Pennine Way and drop down to the old clapper bridge at Hebble Hole, a bridge of huge slabs of rock across the Colden Water. Like Lumb Hole, it provides a very pleasant and sheltered spot for a stop.

Return up the stone path, bearing right along the Calderdale Way and not straight up the Pennine Way. Pass the stile where you joined the stone path and keep on into Fostor Wood. Where the Calderdale Way bears left over the step-stile, you bear right and take the lower path to stay in the wood. The path descends towards the stream and takes you through another beeches and boulders wood. To the right ahead there is a dramatic cliff-edge with Heptonstall church peeping round it.

The path reaches a track which climbs to the left and descends to the right. You climb. Follow the track along the edge of the wood, up to where a track bears left (don't take it) and then down a little. The valley curves round impressively and the church tower is up ahead.

Where the track turns back downhill to the right, you must,. of course, climb the steps on the left, out of the wood and up the field. By a remarkable coincidence, a yaffle laughed as we climbed these steps too. Or was it following us to mock? Through the stile at the top, turn right along the path between walls, with a fine view down into Calderdale.

"... a bridge of huge slabs of rock across the Colden Water ..." – Hebble Hole

Descend gently but do not bear right. Maintain your level and then climb up the road. Before the road turns left, go through the gap in the wall on the right with a Calderdale Way waymark. (If you are not sure of your head for heights, stay on the road and, at the T-junction, turn right into Heptonstall.)

The path ahead is an exciting one, narrow, with rock-scrambling among trees, and then it emerges onto a cliff-edge with a very considerable drop very close (about 600 feet actually). When there is a very strong wind blowing, as on my last visit, one needs to be very careful, particularly as the terrific view from Eaves Rocks over to Stoodley Pike and down onto the gathering of road, river, railway and canal far below in Calderdale is not to be missed.

After a flight of steps comes up from the right, turn left with the Calderdale Way sign, away from dangerous declivities and between new stone houses, a recent addition to Heptonstall. When you reach the older houses, turn left towards the church. Keep to the right of the Victorian church, past Chantry House, and then up the steps on the left (with a sign to the museum) to the old church.

Turn left into the churchyard to look round the ruined church, gaunt, roofless and slightly sinister, return to the gate, and then turn left to the Old Grammar School, a super little museum. Beyond it an angel will greet you before you pass through the archway ahead and out into Towngate.

". . . the ruined church, gaunt, roofless and slightly sinister . . ." – Heptonstall

Turn right down Towngate and continue down the road to leave the village, until, opposite a bench, you can go through the gap in the wall on the left where there is a sign marking the route of your footpath down into Hebden Bridge. A steep, stepped path, with excellent views over the town, takes you down to a road. There you turn right and, before it begins to climb, you bear left down the Buttress, the original road between Heptonstall and Hebden Bridge, not to be attempted in ice and snow. If you can't understand why, you're not safe to be on any of these walks but should just stay at home and read this book in the security of an armchair!

The Buttress brings you to the Old Bridge of Hebden Bridge, dating from 1510, with its interesting inscriptions. Your route back to the station is now up to you. You may be tempted by places of refreshment (tea-rooms, of course), but, if you turn right along Bridgegate, you'll find the excellent information centre on the corner, and you can then turn left along New Road back to train or car.

Gibson Mill to Midge Hole and Hebden Bridge

To return down the valley to Midge Hole and Hebden Bridge, by an energetic route, do not cross the bridge at Gibson Mill but continue along the right bank, up the track until it turns back to the right. Then keep on along the rising path (not up the steps!). The path climbs gently to a grove of beeches and there are constant views through the trees to the hills across the valley.

Then the path climbs steeply, up steps, to the edge of the trees and keeps near the woodland margin, past a spring emerging from the roots of a tree. When the path divides, do not go up the 8 or so steps to the fence but down to the left. Keep on ahead at the junction by the holly bush, and climb gently again to where a walled track goes over the fields to the right. Again keep on down the valley and, at the fork, keep left to descend beneath a contorted oak.

Care is needed as the path is steep in places. It pursues a course along and down the hillside, bringing you out on a track above a reservoir. Turn right along the track and, just past the stone house of Hawdon Hall, bear left down the footpath to descend to Midge Hole.

To finish the walk in Hebden Bridge, turn right through the car park before the bridge, mind the blue pigs, and, at the junction of paths, bear right uphill away from the river. The path, now with a wall on its left, crosses a track, but you turn left along the track, from which views of Hebden Bridge appear ahead.

When you can see the track's junction with the road before you, bear left down the path through the wood, right along the next path for a few yards, and ahead down the stone path between the buildings. Keep on the level path beyond the houses, to look across to the double-deckers of Hebden Bridge, an astonishing sight, and then, where the path turns right uphill, take the curving stepped path left down to the packhorse bridge. Now it's your outward route up the road ahead, right along the main road and left to the station.

For an easier route from Gibson Mill to Midge Hole, cross the bridge at Gibson Mill and follow the riverside path downstream to the right. Keep on the path that stays nearest to the river and is rarely more than about 30 feet above it. Note that, at the third set of stepping-stones (or "hippins", as they are known locally), the path turns away from the river before resuming its customary route. You arrive at Midge Hole through a gap in the parapet of the bridge over the Hebden Water. To return to Hebden Bridge, either follow the route described above or reverse your outward route, which is perhaps a little easier.

Midge Hole to Gibson Mill

Go through the gap in the parapet of the bridge by the lower car park and walk upstream, with the Hebden Water on your left. The path rises and falls a little, sometimes 30 or so feet above the water, but keep to the path nearest the river's edge. The most obvious wildlife the last time I walked along here consisted of mallard, dogs and the dogs' owners.

The path leads you over rocks and roots, through stands of tall pine trees, and sometimes is almost in the river; it's most enjoyable. Pass the outflow from the mill leat, note the apt quotation on the rock in the river, and arrive at Gibson Mill. For Heptonstall or the energetic route back to Midge Hole, cross Gibson Bridge and turn left up the rising track.

Heptonstall to Midge Hole

As you descend Towngate, turn left into Northgate and then, just after Northfield, bear right down Northwell Lane, past the remains of the stocks, on the route of the Calderdale Way. Continue downhill past a cottage (do not fork right) and across the road. Follow the path down through the wood, over a track, and down the path with a wall on the right. You reach the bank of the Hebden Water and follow it upstream to the lower car park at Midge Hole.

2. CAUSEYS AND CURSES

Todmorden – Withens Gate or Lumbutts – Stoodley Pike – Mankinholes
– Todmorden.

Distance: between 3 miles and $8^1/_2$ miles.

Starting Point:

Todmorden railway station; Outdoor Leisure Map 21, South Pennines,
map reference 935243

How to get there:

By car – to Todmorden on the A6033 between Rochdale and Halifax. As
you enter Todmorden, shortly after crossing the Rochdale Canal turn up
to the left to the railway station, where there is a car park.

By train – to Todmorden on the Manchester to Halifax line.

Roads in the Peak District and Lake District were blocked by snow and
we hoped to find some in the South Pennines, but we were most
disappointed to arrive at Todmorden and see none. However, a quick
climb out of the depths of Calderdale revealed snow in plenty. We were
soon ploughing our way along hillsides through knee-deep and then
thigh-deep drifts with a frozen crust (no, I'm not referring to our packed
lunch!). The going made for the kind of progress that is punctuated by
alternate cries of delight and curses. It was a landscape covered with
thick cream, delicious in the sunlight, with the climax of the monument
on Stoodley Pike up ahead.

The Pike is the highpoint of the full walk of about $8^1/_2$ miles, quite a
tough walk with the climb, rough ground, and some very wet patches,
but well worth the effort. For here you have a typical South Pennine
town, hillside terraces of farmland, bare moorland, canal towpath, and,
surveying all, the great obelisk on Stoodley Pike, monument to the
Napoleonic Wars. If you want to climb the pitch-black stairs inside for
the view from the balcony, take a torch.

Instead of doing the full walk, you could climb up to Withens Gate and
then, rather than going along to the Pike, drop down a superb stretch of

stone causey, a marvellous feat of path-making, into Mankinholes, to make the walk one of $5^1/_2$ miles. For a walk which avoids all the rough, wet moorland, you could walk from the Shepherds Rest to Mankinholes via Lumbutts with its distinctive water tower (once containing three water wheels, one above the other), and that would make a walk of $4^1/_2$ miles.

All the three walks can be shortened by about $1^1/_2$ miles if, instead of walking along the canal towpath into Todmorden, you catch a bus. You would still feel you'd had a good walk.

" . . . *surveying all, the great obelisk on Stoodley Pike* . . . "

The Walk

With your back to the station exit, bear right down the road (noting 17th- century Todmorden Hall on the right) to the main road and turn right, away from the Town Hall and over the Rochdale Canal. Just past

Walk 2

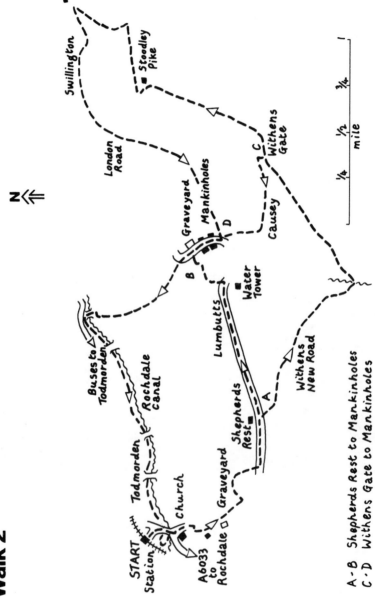

N ⇐

START
Station

Todmorden

Church

A6033
to
Rochdale

Graveyard

Buses to
Todmorden

Rochdale
Canal

Shepherds
Rest

Lumbutts

Water
Tower

A

Withens
New Road

B

Graveyard

Mankinholes

D

London
Road

Causey

C

Withens
Gate

Swillington

Stoodley
Pike

¼ ½ ¾
mile

A - B   Shepherds Rest to Mankinholes
C - D   Withens Gate to Mankinholes

the Golden Lion, cross Longfield Road on the left and go up Honey Hole Road on the route of the Calderdale Way.

Your way is steeply up the road past the magnificent Unitarian church, built in memory of John Fielden, M.P., who instigated the Ten Hours Act in 1847 to reduce workers' hours. Keep beside the churchyard and round the Z-bend of Shoebroad Lane. The centre of the road has a band of setts to stop packhorses slipping – and useful as we climbed in the snow. When we reached the convenient bench, we could look back into sunlit Todmorden, with spire, Town Hall, and railway viaduct, and to the white hills across Calderdale.

Beyond the grey farm at the top of the rise, follow the rough lane ahead. What appears to be a small field on the right of the sett-paved stretch of lane is in fact a Quaker graveyard with tombstones of the 18th to 20th centuries. You can enter via the field-gate at the top, from where you look across the valley to Dobroyd Castle, Victorian home of the Fieldens. Ahead, white cloud concealed the tops of the white hills.

Continue along the lane. Ignore the walled lane leading to the farm on the right and then follow your walled lane round to the left on blocks of stone, a typical South Pennine packhorse trod or causey. Stoodley Pike came and went in the low cloud.

At the T-junction turn right, away from Longfield Farm and up to the road. At the road, turn left towards the Pike again, with super views behind and to the left. The black finger of the monument looked fantastic on its snowy summit and out came my camera – to stay out for the rest of the walk.

Opposite the Shepherds Rest, go through the gate onto Langfield Common (unless you are making directly for Mankinholes, in which case continue along the road). After about 200 yards, where the main track bends left, descend to the track to its left and go along that so as not to climb. The track, Withens New Road, contours round the hillside, boggy in places where neglected since the demise of packhorse trains. At the fork, take the higher track so as not to descend towards the strange water tower at Lumbutts.

The path was not easy to see in the snow but its general course could be discerned round the hillside and it provided super views over Lumbutts and to the Pike. Above a farm you join a fence and wall and keep above them. Your path even turns to the right as it contours around the head of the valley.

The path became narrow (difficult in deep snow) and then disappeared. Stay along the foot of the steep slope, try to keep your feet dry, and a narrow causeway will take you across the main stream. On the far side, head for the Pike again and follow the clear path round the hillside. In 18 inches of snow we lost the path among hummocks of rushes – I suspect you will without the snow – but it reappeared leading round the corner of the hill.

At last (and it really did feel "at last" after struggling through ridges of thigh-deep snow, the 2 miles or so from the Shepherds Rest having taken us one and a half hours) the path turns left above rocks to reach the Pennine Way and arrive at Withens Gate. With relief we enjoyed a rock-seated lunch, looking out over the snow and listening to the rising cries of tobogganing children and sheep – or, to make that clear, perhaps I should say sheep and tobogganing children!

Keep above the rocks and still towards the Pike past a sign that you are on the Pennine Way and crossing the Calderdale Way (where those wishing to descend to Mankinholes turn left down the Calderdale Way). Then pass a large standing stone. The sun was now hidden in cloud, the plateau of Arctic aspect, though a hazy sun later reappeared.

Follow the cairned path through the quarry and along the cliff edge, with the monument growing with every step. The harsh, dark gritstone rocks, blasted clear of snow, contrasted dramatically with their white surroundings. When you reach the monument, you may climb the pitch-dark stair; the descent, in particular, is hazardous without a torch. Even if you don't climb, it is a superb viewpoint for curving Calderdale below you, trapped between the hills. You are at a height of about 1300 feet, some 900 feet above the valley floor.

From the Pike, turn right along the cliff edge, which here changes direction from north to east, and look down on the pattern of fields. You make for a walled plantation, following the cairns and passing a spring debouching into a stone trough. Go through the stile in the wall ahead, over the ladder-stile on the left, and along the path. It bends to the right and descends across the hillside to reach a track at the beginning of the high wall at Swillington Farm.

Turn left along the track, which takes you along the hillside, through a gateway, and over two streams. The track is known as "London Road". It contours round the hillside with magnificent views up Calderdale and over Todmorden, and to the landmark of the tower of Cross Stone church across the valley. Down to your right is a pattern of fields and grey farms, some of them ruins, and up to your left is Stoodley Pike, with the monument soon coming into view.

Try to ignore the rash of modern housing down to the right and look forward to the hamlet of Mankinholes farther along the hillside terrace. Keep above two farms, after which the track can be very wet from all the streams descending the Pike. Once through the gate ahead, the track improves. Keep looking back at the view of the Pike.

When you reach the road at the beginning of Mankinholes, turn right along the road (joined by those who have descended from Withens Gate). The road passes between the interesting and attractive stone houses, an oasis in the wilderness of winter, especially the youth hostel to Pennine Wayfarers. There's an impressive trough to prove it's an oasis for packhorses too. Down to the left is the Lumbutts water tower and up to the right are glimpses of Stoodley Pike.

Opposite the Methodist burial ground a fine paved and walled packhorse track descends to the left (and up it come those who left the main route at the Shepherds Rest). You keep straight on to where the road turns right and leave the road to follow the walled track ahead.

Keep to the left of the barn and follow the right-hand wall to the stone stile beside the gate. Back to the left you can make out your outward route round the hillside and ahead are promises of dramatic views down into Calderdale. Keep beside the right-hand wall and over the next stile.

Now bear left across the field to the next stile, which is in the bottom boundary of the field, about one third of its length from the left and just to the right of a gateway. Over that stile, keep by the left-hand wall to begin the descent into the gorge. You are at about the same height as Cross Stone church, and Heptonstall church is on its hill down the valley to the right.

At the next stile you look down to the left onto the Rochdale Canal and industrial Todmorden, where the Town Hall stands out. Follow the fence ahead and you look down on the railway, road, river and canal all crammed together on the valley floor. This hillside is a good spot for a rest, with the view so full of interest.

Your path descends steeply, goes over the stile at the field corner on the left, and then turns steeply downhill, now keeping the wall on its right. What you need now is a boat on the canal and a train emerging from the tunnel. The path bears left away from the wall, zigzags to the right and then to the left (good, a train of 36 coal wagons has just come out of the tunnel) and finally to the right beside the house which seems to grow out of the hillside. The half-grapefruit scattered about the garden are, according to the owner, to keep cats off the flowers!

" . . . the railway, road, river and canal all crammed together on the valley floor . . . "– Calderdale

Turn down the road to the left and over the canal. On the main road here you can catch a bus to the left to Todmorden, but to finish the walk properly turn to the left along the canal towpath (not back under the bridge).

The River Calder is on your right and on your left a jackdaw-haunted cliff. At the next bridge is a grim, grey gritstone mill and even the variety of ducks can't make the canal beautiful. Cross a towpath ford, pass a lock, another ford and a bridge, and you are approaching the centre of Tod. After a night of heavy rain, I really needed the plank-bridges across the fords the last time I walked along here, as water was pouring across the towpath, and the Calder was a raging brown and white torrent.

Just before the next lock, with the tower of Dobroyd Castle on the hill ahead, you can turn right across the car park into town. However, it's more interesting to stay on the towpath to the next bridge where a horse-tunnel will take you under the road to the top of Todmorden lock. Turn back to the road, left along it, and left up Rise Lane to the station.

If you've time to look round the town, enjoy the punning name of the hairdressers', "Sweeney's of Tod", a walk-justified baked potato with cheese and pickle at "The Coffee Club", and the fine view from the station platform over the Town Hall roof to Stoodley Pike.

Shepherds Rest to Mankinholes

Continue along the road towards Stoodley Pike, keeping straight on down into Lumbutts, with the water tower on your right. After crossing the stream below the tower, and before the road bends right, turn left up the fenced path with the Calderdale Way sign.

At the top of the path (with the Top Brink pub to your right), aim to the right of the house ahead. A walled causey then leads you towards Stoodley Pike again until you reach the road opposite the graveyard. There turn left along the road (with those walking the other routes) unless you wish to make a diversion to look at Mankinholes.

Withens Gate to Mankinholes

At the Pennine Way/Calderdale Way signpost, turn left down the paved path, which curves to the right and then turns back to the left. You look down on the two reservoirs at Lumbutts, across Todmorden, and up the Cliviger Gorge. The path descends to the corner of a wall and continues downhill beside it to two gates and two stiles. Here leave the causey and take the walled track on the right into Mankinholes, where, together with those who've been to Stoodley Pike, you make your way along the road ahead.

3. TRACKS AND TRODS

Littleborough – Summit – Allescholes – Walsden – Blackstone Edge – Littleborough.

Distance: between 4 miles and 12 miles.

Starting points:

Littleborough railway station; Outdoor Leisure Map 21, South Pennines, map reference 938163.

Walsden railway station; Outdoor Leisure Map 21, South Pennines, map reference 933222.

How to get there:

By car – to Littleborough on the A58 3 miles north of Rochdale, and turn right across The Square to the railway station, where there is a car park.

– to Walsden railway station about 4 miles north of Littleborough on the left-hand side of the A6033 between Littleborough and Todmorden. There is no car park at the station, so turn right opposite the station and there is room to park beyond the canal.

By train – to Littleborough on the Manchester to Halifax line.

– to Walsden on the Manchester to Halifax Line.

Not only is this a fascinating and exciting walk but, if you are interested in experiencing the history of transport, it is a revelation.

This walk gives you the opportunity, both in and above Summit Pass (a great gorge cut through the Pennines to a depth of 300 feet and a width of half a mile by glacial meltwater), to follow successive trans-Pennine routes. The track on Blackstone Edge may be a Roman road but is more likely a packhorse track on the route of a Roman road. Later in time, but all on your route, come: packhorse tracks probably dating from the Middle Ages (and subsequently flags); paved with a trod or causey of single or double lines of stone flags: the Rochdale Canal completed in 1804; the Calderbrook and Todmorden Turnpikes with their toll house;

the Manchester and Leeds Railway with its Summit Tunnel, the longest in the world when completed in 1840; and finally, as man reverts to his primitive condition, the first Long Distance Footpath, the Pennine Way.

Add to all that a landscape which is magnificent and dramatic, if not always pretty, and you've a great walk, the full distance being 12 miles with two considerable ascents. The full walk does include a $3/4$ mile stretch over rough, pathless moorland where a compass is useful, so I suggest that should be for experienced walkers.

However, the outward part of the walk, above the west side of the pass, is well marked. When you reach the valley floor again, after about 4 miles, you could catch a bus back to Littleborough or turn north along the canal towpath to Walsden station for a walk of 5 miles. Or you could use the towpath to return through the pass to Littleborough, a total walk of about 8 miles. Instead, you could start from Walsden station and do the tougher, longer second part of the walk, about 9 miles back to Littleborough, or, for an easy, sheltered, interesting walk of 5 miles, follow the canal from Walsden to Littleborough.

I do recommend the full walk for all its interest, and, if you want to learn more about what you have seen, pop into the Coach House Heritage Centre before you leave Littleborough.

The Walk

By Littleborough railway station, go through the subway under the line away from the town centre and turn left along the road. Where the road bends left, keep straight on along the canal bank and up past the first lock.

As you emerge above the second lock, the hills on which you will be walking appear ahead. You pass a third lock and the newly-improved towpath provides a brisk walk, needed on my last visit when there was thick ice on the canal and it was so cold that I could write my notes only by keeping my pen inside my shirt when not in use. By the time you reach the fourth lock the hills of Summit are near.

Continue along the towpath on the left of the canal past the mill buildings. Just beyond the point where the River Roch crosses the railway in a trough, you can turn left across the car park to the road.

Walk 3

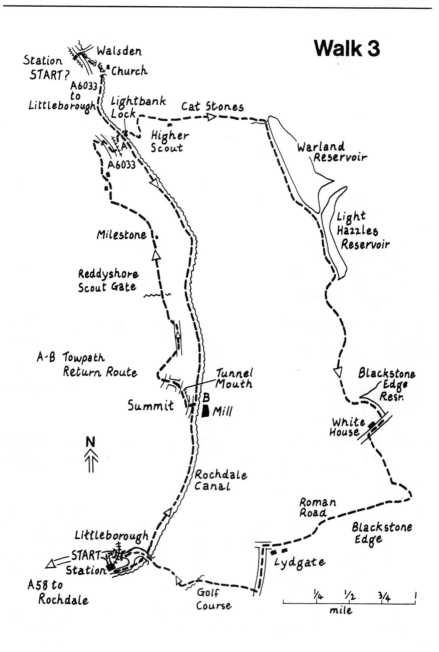

Station START?
Walsden
Church
A6033 to Littleborough
Lightbank Lock
Cat Stones
Higher Scout
A6033
Warland Reservoir
Milestone
Light Hazzles Reservoir
Reddyshore Scout Gate
A·B Towpath Return Route
Tunnel Mouth
Blackstone Edge Resr.
Summit
B
Mill
White House
N
Rochdale Canal
Roman Road
Blackstone Edge
Littleborough
START Station
A58 to Rochdale
Golf Course
Lydgate
¼ ½ ¾ 1
mile

Cross the road and you can look down on the dramatic entrance to Summit Tunnel. Turn left for a few yards towards Littleborough and then turn right up the bridleway and between the wooden bollards. Follow the main path as it curves right between the spoil-heaps.

When you reach the road, with weavers' houses to the left, continue straight ahead up winding Mawrode. At the next road junction, go up the bridleway ahead towards the white-painted house. From that house, look back across the valley to the hills where you will be on the second

" . . . *the dramatic entrance to Summit Tunnel* . . ."

part of the walk, with the prominent rocks on Blackstone Edge, and then bear right up the road.

When it forks, bear right, not between the white gateposts. The road descends and becomes narrow and rougher, turning into a packhorse track with some stone surfacing. Down to the right is a ventilation shaft from Summit Tunnel. Just before you reach the road, you descend one of the country's best stretches of "improved packhorse track", improved from a single trod to a double one to take carts.

At the road, the Calderbrook Turnpike which succeeded the packhorse track as a route from Lancashire to Yorkshire, bear left past the next ventilation shaft. As I passed, I was surprised to hear the noise of a train as it went through the tunnel.

By the next ventilation shaft, leave the road and turn left up the rough track. This gives magnificent views down onto the canal and the latest road (possible to construct only after the canal had drained the valley) as they snake through the pass, the opposite side of which is dramatically man-mauled.

Where the track curves to cross the stream, you can look down into a ventilation shaft, and it's here that you leave Greater Manchester for West Yorkshire. You have also crossed the watershed between streams flowing to the Irish Sea and those flowing to the North Sea.

As you climb up from the stream, there is again a surface of stone slabs for you are on the packhorse track of Reddyshore Scout Gate. At the junction of the two roads below, the Calderbrook and Todmorden Turnpikes, is Steanor Bottom Toll House, built there to catch travellers on both roads.

Electricity pylons march majestically across the hilltops and the cables hang in a great catenary across the gorge. In the quarry just before the pylon, the concrete slab marks the site of the ventilation shaft below which the tunnel fire was in 1984 after a tanker train set alight. My wife and I were two of the 6000 or so who walked the fascinating $1^3/_4$ miles through the tunnel the day before it was reopened to trains. We could see that the heat had been so great that it had vitrified part of the brick lining of the tunnel.

Ahead now are the hills above Todmorden and, just to the left of the mast on the skyline, the weird rocks of the Bridestones. Look out for the Allescholes milestone on the right of the path, giving the distances and directions to Burnley, Rochdale, Todmorden and Halifax, for here there was a junction of packhorse tracks.

" . . . here there was a junction of packhorse tracks . . . " – Allescholes

Not far beyond, the track becomes a walled lane and takes you towards Walsden, ahead in the valley bottom. Keep on the road as it descends past the down-market house and then the up-market one. Walsden comes fully into view with a railway tunnel entrance, a wide stretch of canal, and the mill-owner's mansion from which to survey his empire.

The road swings left round the hillside to a bench. Here you take the path descending back to the right, again with a stone-slabbed surface, to rejoin Allescholes Road, and continue down it to the main road. Cross the road and turn right as far as the first cottage, where you can either catch a bus back to Littleborough or turn left down the footpath immediately beyond the cottage.

Descend the steps to cross the stream by bridge and the railway by level crossing. In the field, bear left and then walk between ditch and wall to the canal towpath near Lightbank Lock, where you turn left for Walsden station, but otherwise you turn right as far as the bridge. Now, with those who started from Walsden, you must choose between the high-level and low-level return routes, with the low-level continuing along the towpath.

For the more exciting and energetic return route, cross the bridge and climb the narrow path alongside the wall ahead, round behind the house, through a wicket-gate, up a stretch of walled path, and then bear left uphill to reach a narrow, flagged path. Turn left up it. I think it is a most atmospheric path, a stretch of packhorse track (or trod, or causey) not improved for carts, and I can well imagine trains of packhorses ascending it.

When you reach the gate, turn and look back through the gorge for the view, and then, through the gate, keep on by the left-hand wall. Just before the white house, you reach a track and turn right up it to continue climbing towards the Pennine Way.

The track leads to Higher Scout Farm with its fine view back across the valley. Keep just to the left of the farm, and then climb the Cat Stones rocks beyond the end of its field wall. There are paths but I suspect that, except at the beginning, they are only sheep-tracks. My best advice is to aim due east and always ascend. There is a helpful pointed cairn to aim for and you continue climbing beyond it to a pair of flat-topped rocks.

The level dam round Warland Reservoir should be visible ahead to the right and you keep on towards the left-hand end of it. You should arrive at the north-west corner of the reservoir by a bridge over an outfall stream. You are now on the Pennine Way.

Turn right along the waterworks track on the dam. As we strode along on our last visit (Wainwright says you can make 4 m.p.h. on this bit of the Pennine Way), on our left the icy surface of the reservoir looked beautiful under the clear blue sky, ahead the sun was reflected off frozen Hollingworth Lake, behind us Pendle Hill poked up on the skyline, and to the right across the gorge was our morning route. The previous occasion when my wife and I had been here, the wind was so strong that we feared we should be blown into the water through gaps in the wall.

Where the dam bears left, you leave Yorkshire. Warland Reservoir is followed by Light Hazzles Reservoir and you keep on the track as it swings along the hillside. To the left are interesting rocks, the summit rocks of Blackstone Edge are ahead, down to the right is Upper

Chelburn Reservoir and, if visibility is good, Hollingworth Lake becomes ever clearer. There are views right across Greater Manchester, and even Winter Hill may be visible beyond Bolton to the west.

Finally, the dam of Blackstone Edge Reservoir brings you to the A58. You turn right, past the White House pub (quickly past in my case), and continue along the next stretch of the Pennine Way by turning left up the signposted path opposite the black and white stone. The route climbs up onto a waterworks path again (positively the last real climb of the day except that onto the platform at Littleborough station) and you turn right along the path beside the drain.

The rocks of Blackstone Edge and the waters of Hollingworth Lake look both impressive and attractive. The path brings you to the "Roman Road", its stones being obvious both uphill and downhill. Do not continue through the wicket-gate ahead but turn right down the stone track. Enjoy the views as you descend and inspect the stones of the causey.

The main road approaches the path but, when you cross the farm drive, bear left to the wall and follow the path downhill alongside it, twisting round hummocks and then by a stream.

You arrive at the row of cottages and farmhouse of Lydgate and beyond them turn left up the walled lane beneath the power line. Where the lane forks, bear right and go through the kissing-gate beside the left-hand gate and follow the track along the edge of the golf course. They know what their members are like and warn of the danger of golf balls!

Where the track turns right, keep straight on by the wall and then across the fairway ahead to the kissing-gate and over the stone-slab bridge. The path then follows the valley to the left, over the footbridge, along by the stream, to the right of the fence round the house, right again, and down the steps to the road.

Follow the road down the Ealees valley, past the half-square of cottages, over the canal and down to the main road. Turn left along it, under the railway and to the left of the parish church back to the railway station. The Coach House Heritage Centre is just up the street on the right after the parish church – and contains seats for sitting on to reduce the weight on your feet!

Walsden to Lightbank Lock

From the Halifax-bound platform of Walsden Station, cross the footbridge, built over a stream. Cross the main road by the zebra-crossing provided especially for you, and go up the road opposite as far as the bridge over the canal. Do not cross the canal but turn right along the towpath between grey, gritstone mills.

You pass Travis Mill Lock, Nip Square Lock and Winterbutlee Lock, with the gorge now ahead and the railway just down to your right. Shortly before the next bridge and lock, the route of the main walk comes in from the right. You continue up the bridge and turn left over it, before Lightbank Lock (unless you're just walking along the towpath into Littleborough).

Lightbank Lock to Walsden

When you reach the canal, with Lightbank Lock just to the right, turn left along the towpath, past interestingly-named locks and Walsden church. Look how the tow-ropes have cut into the abutment of the bridge beyond the church. From the bridge by the next lock, you can see Walsden station to your left. So make for the near platform for trains to Littleborough and Manchester (or the near side of the main road for a bus back to Littleborough if your car is there and it's a long wait for a train).

Lightbank Lock to Littleborough by towpath

To return from Lightbank Lock to Littleborough along the towpath, continue along the canal, ascending at each lock, looking out for Steanor Bottom Toll House across the road on the right, and then descending back into Greater Manchester. It is pleasant and undemanding. You rejoin your outward route at Summit and just keep along the towpath and then the final stretch of road to Littleborough station, where you turn right through the subway under the line.

If you wish to visit the Coach House Heritage Centre, from The Square in front of the station, turn right along the main road and then left up the street before the church.

4. SHADY AND STATELY

Whalley – Wiswell – Sabden – Read – Whalley.

Distance: between 5 miles and 13 miles.

Starting points:

Whalley bus station; Pathfinder Map 680, Longridge and Great
Harwood, map reference 733363 (or Landranger Map 103, Blackburn and
Burnley).

Whalley Road/Clitheroe Road junction, Sabden; Pathfinder Map 680,
Longridge and Great Harwood, map reference 779375 (or Landranger
Map 103, Blackburn and Burnley).

How to get there:

By car – to the junction of the A680 and A671 between Great Harwood
and Clitheroe and then (a) for Whalley turn left along the B6246 and, in
the centre of Whalley, turn left to the car park, or (b) for Sabden turn
right and, in the centre of Sabden, turn right to the car park.

By bus – from Manchester to Whalley bus station, but the service is of
less than hourly frequency, as is the bus from Whalley to Sabden.

By train and bus – by train from Manchester to Blackburn and then by
bus to Whalley bus station. For Sabden, then by bus, of less than hourly
frequency, from Whalley to Sabden.

The sweet, high voices of young children singing hymns from the top of
the tower of Whalley church on a May morning gave a magical effect to
the start of this walk on one occasion when I did it. Both church and
abbey at Whalley deserve a visit at the beginning or end of this walk in a
most attractive area between the Rivers Ribble and Calder and Pendle
Hill. It offers quiet valleys, riverbank, four climbs to ridges, super
woodland including a particularly pleasurable wood called Shady
Walks, and the park of a stately home, Read Hall, built about 1820 with
a bow-window rising to a dome.

The full route, with four climbs, is 13 miles in length, but you can avoid one of the climbs (and miss the pleasant village of Wiswell) on the medium walk of 12 miles. There is also a shorter circuit of 7 miles. By using the infrequent bus service between Whalley and Sabden you could turn the full walk into two linear walks, out to Sabden and back to Whalley, of 5 and 8 miles respectively, but do check the bus times.

There is the echoing stone to try (or is that anti-social?), the peaceful upper valley of Sabden Brook to appreciate, and then that last steep descent into Whalley to look forward to!

The Walk

From the car park or bus station in Whalley, walk along the main street towards Clitheroe (that means away from the steep hill of Whalley Nab) as far as the road on the left for Mitton. Opposite the junction, turn right along Brookes Lane. At the fork, do not turn left into the farm or turn right over the bridge, but keep on the track with the stream on the right. You can look across to the right to the Nab, near the end of the walk.

When the track ends, go over the stile and then uphill, beside the length of fence on the right and parallel to the left-hand side of the field. The path is clear on the ground as it bears slightly right away from the main road, with Whalley viaduct and Longridge Fell back to the right. Then the path bends to the left to a stile.

Over the stile, the path turns right parallel to the road and brings you to a junction with traffic-lights. Cross the road on the left to the entrance to Spring Wood Picnic Site (which has public conveniences in case you forgot to go in Whalley). Turn right along the road as far as the gap in the stone wall of the golf course. Go through, bear left to the edge of Spring Wood, and walk uphill along the side of the wood.

Not far beyond the end of Spring Wood, a sign directs the footpath, and you, left over a footbridge and stile. In the field beyond, bear right between the second and third trees from the left and then uphill alongside the fence on the left. The oaks look sound enough, but the corpses of two giants lie to your right. At the top of the field you have a super view back to Whalley Nab and down the Ribble Valley and you can listen to the cries of the lambs. In the distance to the left, you may discern Darwen Tower on its hill.

Walk 4

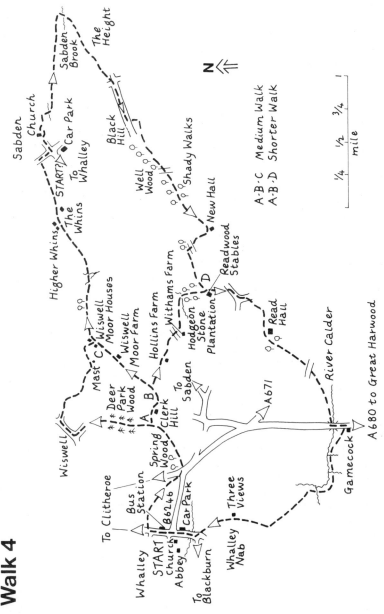

Climb the stile on the left and follow the wall up to the next stile and over it. Do not climb the stile on the right (as the middle and shorter walks do); instead bear slightly left away from the fence. Then follow the fence to the left of the sheep pens, full of frantic, fretting sheep when I was last here, and along the left side of the fence ahead to pass under the power-line.

You come to two stiles and two gates at the edge of the wood. Climb the farther stile, to the left of the farther gate, and take the path stretching ahead through Deer Park Wood, but don't miss the fine view back to Whalley Nab before the trees engulf you. The path through the scented trees is a delightful one and it's almost a pity that you don't need to use the excellent step-stile in the wall ahead. Beyond the gateway, keep on through the wood, where chattering magpies seemed determined to drown all other birdsong.

When you reach the gate and ladder-stile at the far end of the wood, you can see ahead to Clitheroe Castle on its rock and the cement works beyond, with Waddington and Grindleton Fells the hills on the far side of the Ribble valley. Bear slightly left down the field towards the house and barn, over the stile between them, and through the gate beyond beside the footpath sign.

Now turn left down the road into Wiswell. When you reach the road in the village, your route turns right, but, if you make a diversion up the lane opposite, you'll find the Freemasons Arms. On the walking (as opposed to the drinking) route, continue up the road, past the Old School with its war memorial, to Moor Side Lane, on the right just before the end of the village. Turn right up it to begin your climb over Wiswell Moor.

At the top of the metalled road, bear right over the stile or through the gates beside the right-hand lamp and ascend the sunken track, through the trees and beside the stream, with views of Whalley to the right. Soon you can look down on Wiswell and, beyond, to the fine church at Mitton, to Kemple End where Longridge Fell drops down to the Hodder valley, and up the Hodder on its way to join Ribble and Calder near Whalley.

The radio mast on Wiswell Moor comes into view ahead and you continue uphill, near to the right-hand edge of the field, to the corner with two stiles. With most of the climbing done until you are beyond Sabden, and with extensive views up and down the Ribble valley, this is a good spot for a stop. Then climb the left-hand stile and keep by the wall on the right to the next stile, from where the Calder valley and Darwen Tower may be visible. A locomotive crawled across Whalley viaduct; can you count the number of arches? Try 53!

Now bear left towards the pair of gateposts and join the track between them from the mast. Ahead is The Rough, a high point on the ridge leading up to the mass of Pendle Hill, and you can look up the Sabden valley and over the village. On the far side of the valley is wooded Black Hill on your return route.

The last time I was here, I was chatting to an old farmer as he dug up thistles. He told me that, 70 years earlier, his father had brought him up here to show him the echoing stone – and he took me to it and demonstrated its mysterious properties. The stone is the rock on the right of the track not far beyond those gateposts. Stand beside the rock, face The Rough, and shout: the peace of Sabden will be shattered.

Swiftly follow the track downhill, round to the right and through Wiswell Moor Houses Farm to the track to Pendle Hill. Turn left along it, with the medium walkers who avoided Wiswell. Over the stile beside the gate across the track, bear right to keep to the right of the power-line post, and aim for the right-hand end of the wood and Sabden village. There is a stile to the left of the gate ahead. Over that, keep by the edge of the wood on the left and over the stile beside the next gate.

The path keeps to the right of the stream and along the right-hand side of the hummock. It becomes a more obvious sheep-track descending between gorse bushes and turning left to a bridge across the stream. On the far bank, keep on the sheep-track as it maintains its level round the hillside. Cross another stream by stone slabs, towards a mill chimney in Sabden, on beside a little hawthorn, and then to a gateway to the left of a single tree in the wall ahead. A concerned curlew called constantly.

Climb the fence in the gateway and keep straight on towards Pendle Hill, parallel to the wall on the left. Climb the stile at the left-hand corner of the wood and keep on ahead along the sunken track beside the stream and through the stile to the right of the farm buildings.

Keep on the track ahead, between Higher Whins and The Whins, follow it round to the right, and then go through the gate on the left or over the stile beside it. Bear right and follow the right-hand hedge up the field to its top right-hand corner. There go through the very Victorian metal wicket-gate. Sabden church is not very far ahead. Follow the path near to the right-hand fence and out onto the road in Sabden.

Turn right downhill. If you are desperate, Sabden offers seats, refreshment, toilets, and the occasional bus back to Whalley. All those facilities are near the junction of Whalley and Clitheroe Roads in the centre of Sabden, and from there you turn left up Wesley Street towards the parish church. At the top of the street, go through the gateway and up the drive to the neo-Norman church. This is not of great interest, but round its right side is something which may be of more interest – seats for sitting on. There are also some fine rhododendrons, a view to Black Hill, and some of the most impressive watershot masonry I know. The carefully-angled stones give the impression that the wall is leaning outwards, but you can also see that, if the mortar wears away, water will not penetrate the horizontal joints.

Go round to the left at the far end of the church and through the gate to the lane by Sabden House, with an impressive barn to the left. Turn right along the lane and through the wicket-gate beside the gate across the track. In the field, follow the hedge round to the right, cross the stream (perhaps best forded a little upstream) and join the track.

You now turn left up the valley and follow the track with the hills called The Height on your right, in order to have the gentlest possible climb to Black Hill. You pass a reedy reservoir, the home of mallard and their cheeping ducklings.

Cross two cattle-grids, pass a step-stile in the wall on the left, and then look out for the first tree on the right-hand edge of the track. Beside it, descend to the footbridge with handrail. Having crossed it safely (its main plank looks a bit the worse for wear), turn right to keep a little to the right of the stone wall which points towards you. Walk parallel to that wall and make for the step-stile near the far end of the wall at the foot of the steep slope.

Climb the step-stile and follow the path to the right, but I'm going to stop here for my lunch. I usually seem to reach here at the right time when I do this walk and, as I eat, I can sit and look out over this peaceful valley, with no road and the loudest sounds those of larks, lambs and curlew. A heron has just flown down the valley and the flanks of Pendle look superb under the white-cloudy blue sky. Sabden church clock gently strikes the quarters.

Hunger and the temptation to remain here having been conquered, follow this pleasant hillside path along the foot of the moorland, through a rocky patch, to a gap-stile in the wall ahead. Beyond that, keep to the left of the wall with the tree, the steep part of the ascent visible to its right. At the corner of the wall, above Dry Corner Farm, keep on along the hillside so as not to lose height, and join the ascending path, with fine views back up the valley. Cut into the hillside, it looks like an old route you're following, doesn't it? Sabden is well below you, with the road beyond climbing up through the Nick of Pendle and down to Clitheroe.

" . . . the flanks of Pendle look superb under the white-cloudy blue sky . . . "

Beware of traffic as you descend from the stile at the road junction and take the narrow road opposite, along the ridge towards Read. Leave the road at the beginning of Well Wood by going through the stile on the left and over the wall beyond. It's quite a drop on the far side, not helped on my last visit by a lamb sitting on the bottom step. You can look out to Padiham power station and the disused one at Huncoat, with Hameldon Hill the hump on the skyline beyond.

Turn right along by the wall, with the Calder valley to your left and the wood on your right, until you reach the road after several fields. This is an enjoyably easy stretch of the route.

Across the road, climb the stile into the wood called Shady Walks, and it's as attractive as its name. Thirty paces into the wood, take the right fork in the path, so as not to descend by the wall on the left, and then keep to the path with a low cliff dropping to its left. It's a gorgeous wood, with rhododendrons and a mixture of trees, including some fine beeches. At times you have to bend your head beneath the rhododendrons, but there are glades too – and look at that tall larch bending out over the cliff-edge.

Too soon you arrive at the wall round the wood and keep on ahead by it to its corner, where there's a stile, and you look out over Clayton-le-Moors and Accrington to Oswaldtwistle Moor and the West Pennines.

Over the stile, make for the gap in the trees to the right of the farmhouse roof. These fields usually have a complement of handsome horses. You arrive at a strange stile (it always makes me think of supermarket shelves) beside a gate across a farm drive. Climb the supermarket shelves and continue ahead down the drive almost into the farmyard at New Hall. Before the first building on the right, climb the stile on the right and ascend the path which goes uphill behind the buildings, under the beech trees and onto the top of the rocks, where it turns left and then bears right to a stile in the wall. From there you can look across the Sabden valley to the Wiswell Moor radio mast. Farther to the right along that ridge is the high point of The Rough, and you aim for that, walking parallel to the wall on the right, until you reach the ditch across the field, where you bear left down to the end of the wood. Whalley Nab, your last climb of the day, is to the left.

A step-stile takes you out onto the road and you go through the gap to the left of the gate opposite and along the end of the wood to the next stile. On the far side, turn left along by the wall as far as its corner, and then bear right, downhill, aiming a little to the right of the right-hand end of the nearest farm buildings. Swathes of speedwell brightened the meadow with their blue. Cross a rocky piece of field with gorse bushes and descend to a lone tree in the wall ahead. Just to the left of the tree is a not very obvious – or convenient – stone step-stile. Over it, cross the flattened area ahead to a gate leading into Readwood Stables. Now, together with those doing the shorter walk, bear left up the drive to the road, where a pied wagtail preceded me.

Turn right down the road, with Whalley Nab not looking too far ahead now, and then go left at the road junction. Where the road bends left, turn through the kissing-gate beside the gate on the right and follow the path towards the wall round Read Hall. Over the stile by the gate, turn right along the track, which takes you between farm buildings at the back of the hall, which can be seen to the left, over the wall. Beyond the buildings, follow the drive to the right of the handsome horse-chestnut. The drive curves to the left with views back to the hall and its houses.

Descend between the woods (the one on the right good for bluebells and rhododendrons) and march proudly down the drive, past the columned lodge and between the impressive gateposts. Cross the road with great care, to pass between the less impressive gateposts on the far side.

On your left as you follow the track is Martholme viaduct and, farther to the left, behind Huncoat power station, is Hameldon Hill. The track descends to a garden centre and you follow its access road, with the Calder to the left, up to the main road. Turn left over Cock Bridge and up the road, but, before the Gamecock, turn right through the wicket-gate along the path for Whalley Nab.

Follow the path up over a bank and on across the field ahead above the Calder. The path takes you down to a stile and footbridge over a side-stream close to the riverbank, with a cliff on the far bank and trees on both, a good place for a last stop before Whalley.

Keep along the riverbank, with Whalley Nab to the right above the curve of the Calder, ford a little stream, and climb the path as it makes for the top of the cliff. You walk under splendid beeches crowning the cliff, climb the ladder-stile, and continue along the fenced path above the river. Descend deep steps to a stile and down to a bridge over another side-stream, now back at river-level before your final ascent to the Nab.

Beyond the footbridge, keep between fence and hawthorns, then with the hawthorns on your right, and through the hedge ahead. Turn left on the far side of the hedge to its end, and then turn right along the thin path towards a stone barn on the hillside. The path crosses another bridge of stone slabs, keeps by the hedge on the left, and, at the field corner, goes through a kissing-gate to follow the hedge on the right.

At the end of this field, climb the stile on the right, turn left, and then slant up to the top corner of the field, with the day's climbing mostly over and a fine view back. From the stile, a sunken, tree-lined path, with the original track to its left, leads you up to the first of the houses on the Nab. Ahead to your right are the hill you first climbed leading up to Pendle, the Sabden valley and Black Hill.

Bear right along the drive and right again along Dean Lane at the junction. Enjoy the series of houses which you pass and the succession of views to the right. Beyond the house on the right called "Three Views", with its stables, bear right down the narrow path alongside the wall, with the curve of the Calder finely in view.

The path descends steeply, deep in leaves. At the junction of paths, keep to the right for the views down onto the weir, Whalley and the bridge. Turn steeply down the road to the main road and over the bridge into Whalley. I must confess that, as I cross the bridge, I always hope the Toby Jug Tea Shop, not far along on the right, will be open. I love to finish this walk with their scones and a pot of tea.

If you have the time and energy as you walk up the main street back to the car park and bus station, I recommend you to turn left opposite the Whalley Arms and into the churchyard.

" . . . *turn left* . . . *into the churchyard* . . . " – *Whalley*

Go into the church if it's open and then go out through the archway opposite the west door, turn right into The Square, and left to the Abbey. You can appreciate the magnificence of the Inner Gateway and catch a glimpse of the inside even without paying, and you might even manage the extra quarter-mile to the Outer Gateway before returning for your car or bus.

Middle and Shorter Walks

Having climbed two stiles in quick succession, climb the third, on the right. Keep beside the wall for a few paces and then bear left to round the wall round the houses and gardens of Clerk Hill. Four excited guinea fowl leapt to the top of the wall and stalked along it. Pass the attractive cottage garden and the stone building beyond and turn right through the stile beside the gate, and then left along the drive. There was an almost overpowering smell of garlic above the pale blue of forget-me-nots.

At the road, with a fine view down into the Calder valley and across to Accrington, turn left. You reach the drive to Lower Clerk Hill on the right, with a lane just beyond it. For the shorter walk, turn right down that lane, but for the medium walk continue up the road. The radio mast on the left marks the route of the full walk, and the wooded ridge to your right will be your route later.

At the approach to Wiswell Moor Farm, the road deteriorates, but you keep straight on along it to the next farm, Wiswell Moor Houses, where the full walkers come down from the left. With them, you climb the stile by the gate ahead and follow their route for the rest of the day.

Shorter Walk

From the road, turn right down the lane beyond the drive to Lower Clerk Hill. The lane takes you down to Hollins Farm and you go through the gate ahead to the left of the stone barn. Follow the stony path ahead into a hollow with a stream, across which an ash tree had blown down when I was last here. Across the stream, descend the right-hand edge of the field near the stream. The field is rough underfoot, so be careful if you're tempted to look at the fine view of Pendle Hill to the left.

You arrive at a stile in the fence ahead and continue beside the stream to reach the road by a stile close to the stream. Cross the road and go through the stile directly opposite. Then keep along the right-hand side of the field and go through the gate ahead, with Withams Farm to the right. Now turn left to follow the line of poles and on the left, near the bottom of the field, is a ladder-stile.

Climb it, avoid the concealed ditch on its far side, and keep by the fence on the right, with Sabden Brook on your right. In the fence ahead are a stile and footpath sign. Across the stile and the stream beyond, climb the bank and you will see a footbridge ahead. Cross Sabden Brook by it, and perhaps stop for a break, as it's a pleasant spot.

Then climb with the path up to the wood of Hodgeon Stone Plantation. The path slants up to the right through the trees, a most enjoyable path when bluebells are blooming and curlew calling. When you reach the edge of the wood, bear left to keep the stone wall on your right. Continue along the right-hand edge of the field ahead, from where you can look back to Whalley Nab and your route down into the valley. A stile beside an oak in the fence ahead lets you into the yard at Readwood Stables, where you turn right up the drive with those doing the other walks.

5. GREEN AND GROWING

Ribchester or Ribchester Bridge – Dinckley Bridge – Hurst Green – Stonyhurst College – Hud Lee – Stydd – Ribchester or Ribchester Bridge.

Distance: between $4^1/_2$ miles and 12 miles.

Starting points:

Ribchester Bridge; Pathfinder Map 680, Longridge and Great Harwood, map reference 662356 (or Landranger Map 103, Blackburn and Burnley).

Ribchester; Pathfinder Map 680, Longridge and Great Harwood, map reference 650353 (or Landranger Map 103, Blackburn and Burnley).

How to get there:

By car – on the A666 north from Blackburn to Wilpshire and there turn left along the B6245 to the de Tabley Inn beside the River Ribble. To start from Ribchester Bridge, do not cross the bridge but continue along the minor road and park beyond the bends. To start from Ribchester, cross the bridge, continue along the B6245 to Ribchester and follow the signs to the car park on the left.

By train and bus – by train to Blackburn and then bus to the de Tabley Inn at Ribchester Bridge, but note that the bus service is a 2-hourly one.

When I last did this walk, I was intensely conscious that everything around was green and growing and that woods and hedgerows were full of lush vegetation in almost tropical profusion. It's that sort of area, with streams flowing down wooded valleys into the Ribble, rolling hills, grassy fields and many trees. It's charming country rather than spectacular, and to my mind is one of the loveliest parts of Lancashire.

You might even disagree with me when I say it's not spectacular: witness the views of the Ribble and Pendle Hill, and the wonderful sight of Stonyhurst at the end of its drive. This great 16th-century house of the Shireburns is now a boys' public school run by the Jesuits, and there are other marvellous buildings to be seen on this walk, including Dutton Hall of about 1670 with its bay windows, Stydd Chapel (Norman and Early English) and the delightful almshouses built at Stydd in 1726 for five Roman Catholic widows or spinsters. For details of the buildings you will see, I recommend "Historic Walks around Ribchester" by John Dixon and Jaana Järvinen.

The complete walk from Ribchester bridge is $11^1/_2$ miles, but you could reduce that to 9 miles by omitting the loop from Hurst Green to Stonyhurst. You could have a super stroll along the south bank of the Ribble to Dinckley bridge and back along the north bank – only $4^1/_2$ miles – or you could extend that walk to Hurst Green with its refreshment facilities – 6 miles – or to that walk you could add the loop from Hurst Green to Stonyhurst for a walk of $8^1/_2$ miles.

Ribchester is well worth seeing, the interesting bits being off to the left of the main road, towards the river: church, Roman remains, Museum of Childhood, Village Tea Shop, pubs (especially the White Bull) and old houses. If you are using public transport and want to finish your walk at Ribchester itself, it will reduce the length of the longer walks by half a mile or add about a mile to the shorter walks. Car-travellers wanting to begin and end the longer walks at Ribchester will have an extra half-mile of walking.

" . . . don't bounce up and down on the suspension bridge at Dinckley . . ."

It's such a lovely area that you may want to return and do all the variations of this walk. So, to make sure you can return, don't bounce up and down on the suspension bridge at Dinckley!

The Walk

From the de Tabley Inn, do not cross Ribchester bridge, but walk along the minor road ahead by the river and enjoy the view back to the bridge. As the road curves right, there is a splendid view of Pendle Hill ahead and on the left across the river is the wood through which the shorter walks return.

Lambs, curlew and peewits may be vocally active as you follow the road round to the right, between the house and barns of Salesbury Hall, and then left and uphill into the wood. There go over the stile on the left (the sign says it's 2 miles to Hurst Green) and down the fenced path ahead. The path takes you across a stream. You can now rejoice in one of the most beautiful stretches of footpath in Lancashire, through Sale Wheel Woods and along by the Ribble, with its bleached rocky outcrops and giant hogweed.

All too soon, it seems, you cross a stile and leave the wood, but the delightful path continues along the riverbank and then turns right to follow a line of rocks, once painted white, in a declivity. The next stile brings you back to the riverbank, past damp patches containing wild iris, and very soon within sight of Dinckley bridge with Pendle beyond. Before the bridge is a sandy beach, a good place to stop and watch mallard, pied wagtails, dippers and heron.

Cross the bridge, quite an exciting experience in itself, with good views upstream and down, and keep on the path towards the farm. If you don't want to go to Hurst Green, at the end of the fenced path and before the farm (with a view across the river to Dinckley Hall) turn back sharp left and ascend the cart-track, on the Ribble Way. But for Hurst Green, do not turn left before the farm. Instead, keep straight on between the farm buildings at Trough House, past the piggy smells and noises and the dogs on chains, and up the farm drive. As you ascend, the river and Pendle are through the trees on your right.

You may be glad of the bench strategically placed part-way up the hill, with a view back to the Ribble. Then keep on climbing and the buildings

Walk 5

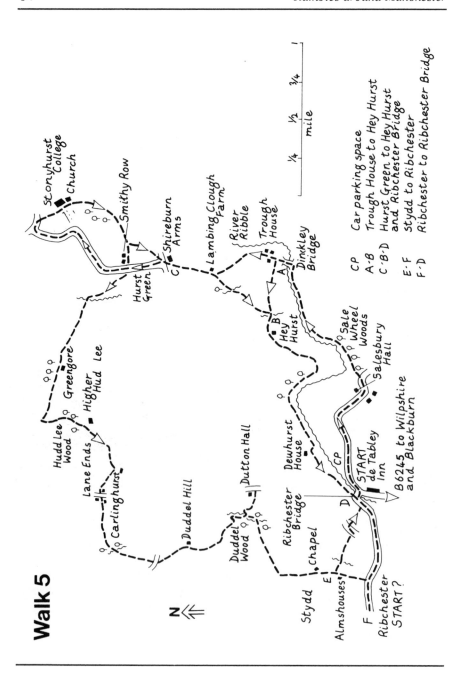

N

Stonyhurst College Church
Smithy Row
Shireburn Arms
Lambing Clough Farm
River Ribble
Trough House
Dinkley Bridge
Hurst Green
A
B
Hey Hurst
Sale Wheel Woods
Salesbury Hall
Greengore
Higher Hud Lee
Hudd Lee Wood
Lane Ends
Carlinghurst
Duddel Hill
Dutton Hall
Dewhurst House
CP
START de Tabley Inn
B6245 to Wilpshire and Blackburn
Ribchester Bridge
Duddel Wood
Stydd Chapel
D
E
Almshouses
F
Ribchester START?

CP   Car parking space
A-B   Trough House to Hey Hurst
C-B-D Hurst Green to Hey Hurst
       and Ribchester Bridge
E-F   Stydd to Ribchester
F-D   Ribchester to Ribchester Bridge

¼ ½ ¾ mile

of Hurst Green quickly appear. As you approach the village, Pendle looks magnificent dominating the view to the right.

You reach Hurst Green beside the Shireburn Arms and there are other sources of provisions and refreshment too, my favourite being the Whitehall café. On one winter visit, a hot, home-made scone just melted in my mouth – and my glasses steamed up! Turn right past the Shireburn Arms and then up the first road on the left, beside the war memorial. Shop, café and Eagle and Child are on the right, and you soon reach public conveniences and the Bayley Arms. A little further up the road are seats, swings and finally the handsome Shireburn Almshouses built in 1706 at the eastern end of Longridge Fell and moved here in 1946. And to fulfil your final need, there's a graveyard a little higher up the road!

For Stonyhurst, continue through the gateway ahead (a little worrying when you're guiding a coach through it) but, if you're avoiding

" . . . you can enjoy the view of the buildings reflected in one of the long ponds . . . "–
Stonyhurst College

Stonyhurst, turn left opposite Smithy Row. So, for Stonyhurst, it's through the gateway and up the road, past the graveyard, to the statue of the Virgin Mary. From the corner of the road there is a striking vista to the facade of Stonyhurst College. Walk towards it (unless that's as far as you're going and you either return to Hurst Green or walk back as far as Smithy Row and then turn right for the rest of the walk).

As you approach Stonyhurst, at the gateway into the grounds turn left with the road and you can enjoy the view of the buildings reflected in one of the long ponds, with its mallard and yellow irises. Follow the road round to the right with attractive glimpses of the school buildings between the trees. At the T-junction, turn right and then keep straight on through the gateway and into the school grounds. It's a private road but a public footpath that takes you between the main buildings and the long ponds, giving close-up views of the house and distant views over the ponds and up the vista of the drive.

The school buildings are not open to the public but the church on the left is worth a look inside. Go round to the far end of the church and in through the far door. The last time I was there, I was able to sit in the gloom of a grey day and listen to the organ being played.

Continue along the drive past the church, and, where it turns left by the observatory, keep straight on through the metal gate and alongside the fence on the left, with a wood to your right. Opposite a kissing-gate on the left, the path veers right towards the wood (there's a view back to the pavilions in Stonyhurst's garden) and then it follows the right side of the field round to a metal kissing-gate.

Through it, keep by the right-hand hedge and through another kissing-gate to a third. To continue the long walk, keep straight on through that kissing-gate to the next one, and follow the path round by the wall of Four Meadows cottage and along Smithy Row to the road junction. (But to return to the centre of Hurst Green, turn left before that third kissing-gate to keep by the hedge on your right. When you reach the stone wall, follow it round to the left and go over the stile beside the gate ahead. Pendle Hill stands up to your left and the cupolas of Stonyhurst College top the trees behind you. The track brings you back into Hurst Green beside the café).

From whichever direction you come to continue the long walk, go along the drive opposite the end of Smithy Row. Then turn right along the upper track, past a bungalow, with a valley to your left and perhaps the sound of the stream rising from it. Where the drive bears right into the trees, take the path ahead.

It leads you gently down to a beautiful spot, where the stream forms pools between little rapids in the shade of lovely trees. Saunter to savour this bit. When I was last here, I met an elderly couple with dog, spade and heavy loads in plastic sacks, very mysterious, but I didn't dare to ask them what they were carrying. Stay beside the stream until you cross it by the stone bridge and have a look at the cataracts just upstream. There's an old stone wall that makes a good picnic spot.

Now bear left uphill, parallel to the old, sunken track, keeping the ruined wall on your left until the path takes you through the wall and you continue between wall and fence to the corner of the wood. Longridge Fell is ahead to your right, Hill Farm is to your left, and tormentil and heath bedstraw are at your feet.

Keep on along the track where, when I last walked this way, there were masses of campion and buttercups, and foxgloves were in flower. There were stitchwort, ragged robin, honeysuckle and ladysmock, and I had to force my way past bracken and willow.

A better track comes in from the left but you keep on to the old, buttressed house of Greengore, with a deep, wooded valley to its right. Continue along the track to the right of the buildings, over the stile, and beside the wall and Deer House Wood. When the wood ends, keep along the track, the crest of Longridge Fell looking quite close now, and make sure you remain near the right-hand edge of the field to arrive at a stile beside a gateway.

Climb the stile and continue past the gorse bushes and across a boggy stretch to a pair of stone gate-posts. Through them, immediately turn left up by the ditch and bank, which you follow as they bend left to the corner of the wood. Go through the gate there into the wood, with a lovely green view back to Longridge Fell.

A thin path leads through the trees, for a short while keeping near the edge of the wood, Hudd Lee Wood. It then ventures more deeply into it, but the edge of the wood is never out of sight to the left. At the end of the wood, climb the stile by the gate and turn right away from the farm of Higher Hud Lee, to the diagonally opposite corner of the field, not along by the woodland edge.

Stones show you where the stile is in the field-corner (20 heavy-breathing cows came to gawp at me over the stile after I had left their field) and the next stile can be seen ahead with the roof of Carlinghurst Farm beyond. Mizzle had blocked out the views across the Ribble valley to the left, and it made everywhere seem so incredibly green., but there was no problem in seeing the stile.

Over that stile, make for the extensive buildings of the farm and follow the track towards it, through the gate, to the farmhouse. There turn right, up the farm drive, to reach the road at Lane Ends. Take the track to the left of the house on the far side of the road, beware of the massed gnomes, and go up the path on the right of the house at the end of the track. Climb the ladder-stile at the bottom of the garden and keep straight on over the stile in the fence ahead and down to a stile between two tiny, tinkling streams.

Bear very slightly right through a gateway and, beyond that, bear slightly left to a stile in the fence ahead, leading into the wood. It's under a rhododendron bush about a quarter of the way down the field from the right. Go over the stile and the path will take you down to the left, through rhododendron thickets, to a drive. Turn left and, immediately over the bridge, go through the kissing-gate on the right. Go up to the lone tree on the skyline. From that tree, descend to the next single tree ahead, keep on in the same line (to the left of the farm buildings) and a stile will appear in the fence ahead. Again, continue in the same line beyond it, to the stile in the hedge on the road corner.

With care, cross the road (the bus route between Preston and Clitheroe) and walk up the farm drive opposite, to Duddel Hill Farm. Follow the drive beside the house (I wonder why the handsome buildings are separate from the house) and on to the solitary tree beyond. Until I entered the next wood, there was a concatenation of cries from anguished curlew which I assume had eggs or young near my path. From this field there is a fine view of the Ribble valley.

Past the tree, continue along a barely-visible sunken track and then bear down to the left keeping on the faint traces of wheel-tracks, just to the right of a hollow, to a gate in the fence ahead. Through the gate, turn left beyond the pond and keep by the left-hand hedge to the stile ahead. Over that, bear right across the field to the ruined building in the far corner.

Climb the stile to the right of the ruin, where tree-roots make an excellent seat and the thick canopy of leaves will ward off a heavy shower in summer, as I know with gratitude after a protected tea-stop. Then turn left along the edge of the field to a stile in the corner. Over that, you descend to the right to join the path in Duddel Wood.

The path soon forks and you take its lower branch down the valley, over a footbridge across a sidestream to a footbridge across the main stream, which you also cross, above rocky slabs in the streambed. The path rises to a junction and the direct route back to Ribchester bridge turns right. (For the very worthwhile diversion to Dutton Hall, turn left and then follow the path as it swings right, round the end of the former millpond of Dutton Mill, up and along the valley side to a stile in the fence on the left. Over the stile, follow the wall up the field, go through the gate to the right of the tank, and turn left and into the forecourt of the Hall for a view through its gate. Then retrace your steps back to the stile and down into the valley to the junction of paths.)

The path down the valley takes you past the stone walls and wheel-pit of Dutton Mill to the next bridge over the stream. Turn right across it and along the clear path ahead to the stile leading out of the wood. Out in the field, bear left to the top corner of the field, with the Ribble and the hills beyond it to the left. Soon even Ribchester bridge is visible to the left.

The next stile is a pair of them to the right of the wood with a pond in it. In the next field (with Ribchester now ahead) you again bear slightly left to pass close to the corner of the field on the left and then to aim for the gable-end of the house ahead. You should arrive at the far side of the field with a gate and stile just to your left.

Go over the stile and down the cart-track near the left-hand fence. Follow the track not into the farmyard but to the stile to the right of the row of conifers and only then into the farmyard, to keep to the left of the house. Dogs barked; the cats merely preened themselves.

You pass the lovely little chapel of Stydd. When I was last there, it was full of the loud voices and learned expressions of a visiting party, one of whom, on seeing me, inquired of her companion, "Are we on the Pennine Way?" I didn't wait for the answer but walked on over the little bridge to the next building of delight, the recently cleaned and restored almshouses.

Having enjoyed them, for Ribchester continue down the drive. To return to Ribchester bridge, cross back over the bridge and turn right along by the hedge, over the stile on the right beside the stream, by the left-hand hedge to the next stile, and over that, round to the left to the footbridge over the next stream. Now keep by the fence on the right and over several stiles until you cross the last, narrow field and up the steps to the road.

" . . . *the next building of delight, the recently cleaned and restored almshouses* . . . " – *Stydd*

Turn left along it (you can look up to the left to Dutton Hall) and look carefully for the stile on the right, perhaps 30 yards after the first gate on the right, as it may be obscured by vegetation. Cross the field to the unusual – and commendable – combined gate and stile in the middle of the far side of the field and turn left along the road to Ribchester bridge. Cross it and turn left for your car or right for the bus stop. If it's some time before the bus is due, you could stroll a little way up the road towards Blackburn to look at the sensitively-restored building of New Hall.

Ribchester to Ribchester Bridge

To start the walk from Ribchester, from the car park return to the main road and turn right along it back towards Blackburn. Cross Ribchester bridge, and turn left along the road with those who have started the walk from the bridge.

Trough House to Hey Hurst

For the shortest walk, not visiting Hurst Green, turn back to the left between Dinckley bridge and Trough House and keep on the cart-track, with good views left to the bridge, and follow the Ribble Way waymarks. When you reach a fence-corner just past a trough, with a pair of metal gates on the left, keep along the right-hand side of the fence and hedge ahead. This will bring you to a stile by a wooden gate, where you keep straight on. The hedge later bends right and brings you to another stile by the next gate. Go over that, again keep to the right of the fence ahead, and you will arrive at a footbridge by the corner of a wood, where the Hurst Greeners will rejoin you.

Hurst Green to Hey Hurst and Ribchester Bridge

For the shorter route from Hurst Green to Ribchester bridge, retrace your steps down Lambing Clough Lane on the right-hand side of the Shireburn Arms, as far as Lambing Clough Farm, the first farm down the lane. Then, immediately after the cattle-grid, leave the lane and bear right across the field to the edge of the wood. In the field-corner ahead you will find a stile, over which you continue downhill to a footbridge. Cross it, and climb up to the stone arch on the right.

Do not go onto it, but turn left along the hillside, keeping just above the two tall firs and along the top of the steep slope on the left. Follow the path above the trees and past the site of a hut, swing right so as not to descend into the side-valley, and go over the stile in the fence to the right of an oak tree.

In the next field, keep on up the side-valley and then turn left between the wood and the end of the hill, where a group of black bullocks stood on the skyline facing me like Red Indians about to charge. They did – and came bouncing around me, but meant no harm. At the end of the wood you reach a footbridge, and there meet those who have come from Dinckley.

All now follow the well-waymarked Ribble Way, almost back to Ribchester bridge. Cross the footbridge and then follow the right-hand side of the field round the corner and up to a stile in its top corner. Cross the drive leading to Hey Hurst, go over the stile a few paces to the right on the opposite side of the drive and bear left to the field gate.

Through that gate, aim for the gateway about a third of the way down from the right in the fence ahead. Go through it, cross the stream, and then make for the dip in the hillside ahead. (If you follow the Ribble Way signs here, you take a shorter route across this field.) As you climb, there is a quite outstanding view back over the river to Pendle Hill. As you descend the other side of the hill, bear right to enter Haugh Wood by a stile near the foot of the slope.

Follow one of the paths through the wild garlic and between the trees round this superb, wide bend of the Ribble, with a good chance of seeing heron at work. A footbridge takes you out of the wood and then keep parallel to the river and along the top of the bank. Keep between the buildings of Dewhurst House Farm and the river and to the left of the fence round the garden. Climb the ladder-stile on the right, walk up by the garden fence into the farmyard and then turn left along the drive to the left of the farmhouse.

The drive brings your walk to an excellent end as it provides a fine view of the river and Ribchester bridge, over which you turn left for car or bus.

Stydd to Ribchester

From the almshouses at Stydd, continue down the drive to the main road and turn right, past the Ribchester Arms (bus stop for Blackburn) and into the centre of the village.

6. CANALS AND CANARIES

Burscough Bridge – Top Locks – Rufford – Mere Sands Wood – Martin Mere – New Lane – Burscough Bridge.

Distance: between 6 miles and 12 miles.

Starting Point:

Burscough Bridge railway station; Pathfinder Map 699, Chorley and Burscough Bridge, map reference 444125 (or Landranger Map 108, Liverpool).

How to get there:

By car – to Burscough Bridge just north of the junction of the A5209 and the A59 between Wigan and Ormskirk. There is a car park at Burscough Bridge railway station (not to be confused with Burscough Junction station!) or, if travelling northwards on the A59, you could, immediately after crossing the canal, turn back sharp left and park by the canal.

By train – to Burscough Bridge on the Manchester to Southport line.

This walk is different from the other walks in this book: it is dead flat!

About half the walk is along canals, the towpath of the main line of the Leeds and Liverpool Canal and its Rufford Branch. It then goes out across the low and level mosslands to visit the canaries. Well, no, that bit of the title is a downright lie. At the Wildfowl Trust at Martin Mere (open every day), you should see a variety of birds, but not canaries. Martin Mere is one of the reasons for the walk, especially in the winter, with thousands of pinkfooted geese and Bewick's and whooper swans, a thrilling sight and sound. Also of real wildlife interest is the Lancashire Trust for Nature Conservation's Mere Sands Wood Nature Reserve, a delightful combination of woodland and open water, with the chance of seeing red squirrels as well as birds. It is always open, and is free, as public rights of way pass through it.

And, if your interest is old buildings, this walk will give you the opportunity to visit the National Trust property, Rufford Old Hall. Or, if you don't pay your money to go round, the canal towpath provides a lovely view of it.

Only in a very long day would you find time to do the full walk and do justice to the two nature reserves and the historic house. The full walk is 12 miles in length (reduced to about 11 miles if you don't go all round Mere Sands Wood), or there is a shorter circuit omitting Mere Sands Wood and Rufford and being 9 miles in length. By catching the occasional bus from Martin Mere back to Burscough Bridge you could reduce all the walks by 3 miles; or, if you caught the train from New Lane to Burscough Bridge or back to Manchester, you would cut each walk by about 2 miles.

So, arithmetic done, boots on, and off you go . . .

The Walk

Leave Burscough Bridge station by the narrow doorway from the Southport-bound platform and follow the station drive ahead, past the car park, and left to the main street. Turn right along the main street until you reach the bridge over the Leeds and Liverpool Canal and there turn right down the steps onto the towpath. Then turn left under the bridge and continue along the towpath past the works with its elegant, cast-iron awning, under the Ormskirk-Preston railway line and on with a view ahead to Ashurst's Beacon, with Parbold and Harrock Hills to its left.

You arrive at Top Locks with its impressive canal signpost, attractive rows of cottages and a dry dock, which had a narrowboat in it on one of my visits. Cross Junction Bridge over the mouth of the Rufford Branch of the canal and turn left along the cobbled path in front of No. 1 Top Locks, behind the Ship Inn (formerly known as the "Blood Tub"!) and along the road beside the canal.

After crossing the road at Runnel Brow Bridge, take the track on the opposite side of the road. Keep to the left of Lock Cottage, along the canal bank and under the Wigan-Southport railway. You pass Moss Lock, Germans Lock before Germans Bridge, and Chicken Lock before Baldwin's Bridge. On one occasion it was strange to be walking along the towpath of the still and silent canal above the utterly flat fields which disappeared into the mist. The modern world seemed distant in

Walk 6

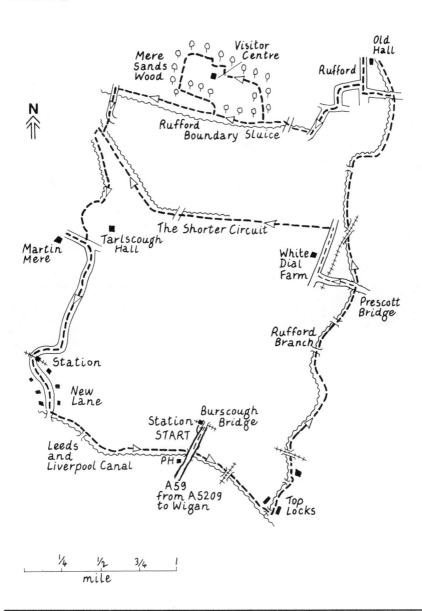

both space and time – it could have been 1816, the date on Junction Bridge, as we spied two men with guns and spaniels, grey figures on our right.

" . . . you arrive at Top Locks . . . "

The next bridge is number 5, Prescott Bridge, where there are sturdy picnic tables on the towpath. Here those walking the shorter circuit leave the towpath.

For the full walk, continue northwards along the towpath, leaving Harrock Hill and its ruined windmill behind you to the right. You pass under the strangely-shaped bridge of the Ormskirk-Preston railway line, perhaps enjoy the gold blobs of the marsh marigolds in the wet wood on the right, and then suffer the proximity of the A59 on the left.

Continue past Marsh Meadow swing bridge, away from the A59 and towards the spire of Rufford church. The towpath swings right and then left to Rufford Lock, just before which, on the right, is a Lancashire and Yorkshire Railway boundary stone.

At the concrete bridge by Rufford church, your route takes to the road and turns left, but it's well worthwhile keeping on along the towpath for a short distance for attractive views of Rufford Old Hall across the canal and between the trees. Then retrace your steps to the bridge and cross it.

The church could hardly be more Victorian (Sir Nikolaus Pevsner in "The Buildings of England" says, "The architects hardly deserve recording.") and then when you discover it's Diamond Jubilee Road. . .!

Just before the A59 junction, look out for the milk churns on the right and then turn right towards Preston. If you don't want to visit the Hall, then turn left into Flash Lane, the first road on the left. Otherwise continue along the main road for the short distance to the entrance, enjoy your visit, and then return to Flash Lane and along it.

Pass the Scout hut and a variety of houses as you follow the road round to the left. At the road junction beyond the school, turn right and then take the third road on the left, Brick Kiln Lane. Opposite the old chapel, take the path on the right on the far bank of the stream. Keep between stream and gardens and out onto the road. Cross both road and stream and go along the drive past the pavilion and along the stream's bank to the corner of Mere Sands Wood.

The direct route goes straight ahead, but do follow the path to the right, just within the edge of the attractive woodland. At the visitor centre, a warden was complaining that the pair of mallard at my feet had eaten all the frogspawn in his pond. Continue across the car park and again the footpath is absolutely clear, keeping just inside the wood and affording access to hides which give good views across the areas of open water. On the spring day when I was last here it was a delight of birds and birdsong, of sunlight coming through the great variety of trees.

When the path divides at Nature Trail point 8, turn right over the bridge so as to continue near the edge of the wood. Only a short distance further on, just beyond point 9 and among beech trees on the woodland edge, you rejoin those who didn't walk all round the reserve and turn right along by the stream and ditch of Rufford Boundary Sluice. (Those who took that shorter alternative will just have kept to the edge of the wood with the stream on the left until they emerged from the trees.)

The last time I took that shorter route the fields on my left were full of shimmering sheets of shallow water – which turned out to be sheets of polythene protecting young plants.

Your course is now dead straight alongside the ditch, with Mere Sands Wood to your right and Woodlands Farm to your left. At the end of that straight march across the landscape, you arrive at a stone bridge and turn left over it and along the road.

Where the road turns left and you keep straight on beside the hedge, you are, according to the map, only 2 metres above sea level, so hope that there is not a very high tide in Southport. You cross the footbridge (which is the second of the two footbridges referred to at the end of the description for those doing the shorter circuit, who rejoin the full route here) and turn right.

All cross the footbridge ahead, with a disused windmill beyond adding to the Dutch impression. On the far side of that bridge, turn left with a ditch on your left to the next stile. Climb the stile, and then bear right across the field, in the direction of the waymark arrow, to a waymark post at the right-hand end of a raised track. If you cannot immediately see the post, aim for the farm of Tarlscough Hall on its slight hill ahead and then make for the post when you can see it.

Bear left along the track with a ditch on the right and Southport's impressive gasholder much farther to the right. Follow the track, turning right by the bush and right again at the junction of tracks. Continue on the track as it curves left past a house (with Tarlscough Hall to the left) and, at the junction of tracks, turn right to the road. Martin Mere is just to the right along the road.

If you want a rest, you can watch birds from inside the visitor centre. It has a coffee shop, and there are semi-wild ducks and geese from all over the world in pens, but the thrilling part is the open water and fields which you can view from hides. These areas are full of life in winter. On my last visit I watched the sky fill with teal and wigeon as the passage of a bird of prey drove them from the water, and three heron flew over too. Many majestic swans were on the water and geese were feeding on the surrounding fields. It was a bitterly cold day and I had one hide to myself, except for a mole which scuttled about my feet.

If you are not wishing to visit Martin Mere, turn left along the road or, if you have looked round, turn right out of the car park and along to where you joined the road. A short distance ahead, turn right down Marsh Moss Lane. On one memorable visit, the sun was sinking through the clouds and the sky was gold, grey and blue, and silhouetted against that backcloth were the lovely shapes of skein after skein of pink-footed geese flighting to their roosts and a marvellous sound filled the air. One of my bird books says, "Flighting pinkfoots are highly vociferous, producing a thrilling cacophony in which the high-pitched voices of males can be distinguished from those of females, which are an octave lower". Yes, thrilling it is.

By the time we reached New Lane railway station that day it was too dark to finish the walk along the canal to Burscough Bridge. So we caught the train from New Lane; it was a relief to see it appearing out of the darkness. But, to complete the walk, keep on along the road as far as the swing-bridge across the canal, and turn left along the towpath, on the near bank.

There are many boats moored here, to add interest to the last stage of the walk. You pass Crabtree swing-bridge with its attendant pub which has, I imagine, a unique name (sorry, you'll just have to go and find out!) and house number 52, which you should be able to recognise. Then stride out along the final stretch of towpath. Climb the steps beside bridge 32A opposite the Admiral Lord Nelson and turn left along the road back to Burscough Bridge station or your car.

The Shorter Circuit

At bridge number 5, Prescott Bridge, climb up to the road and turn left over the canal with the spire of Rufford church poking up over the trees along the canal to the right. The road takes you over the Ormskirk-Preston railway to a thatched house on the busy A59.

Turn right along the road past White Dial Farm with its white sundial and on the house opposite an enjoyable weather vane showing the effects of the local weather – so beware. Then turn left along the track immediately after the sign for Moss Lane (the road you are on), opposite the parish and hundred boundary stone, and waymarked "FP 91". The track pursues an absolutely straight course across the fields, somewhat disheartening if you're walking directly into a bitter, winter wind. In the latter part of its journey while keeping straight on the track runs along the left bank of a drainage ditch beside a line of electricity poles.

On one winter day as we walked we disturbed flocks of feeding pink-footed geese which took to the air and circled before landing again, and there was a dead goose beside the track. The great expanses of sky and the flat land broken by the wintry grey shapes of groups of trees caused my wife to say that it was like walking through a Dutch landscape painting.

We couldn't understand why cars kept stopping on the road ahead, with the drivers leaping out, picking something up off the road, and then driving off. But when we reached the road we found that part of a load of cabbages had been shed along the roadside, so I have to confess that we continued our walk with my rucksack weighed down by a large cabbage that had "fallen off the back of a lorry".

Go straight across the road, with or without cabbage, to continue along the left bank of the ditch, and follow the ditch round the corner to the right, past two footbridges over the ditch on the right. At the second footbridge you rejoin the route of the full walk.

7. FAIRIES AND PHAROAHS

Parbold – Harrock Hill – Fairy Glen – Appley Bridge – Ashurst's Beacon – Parbold.

Distance: between $5^1/_2$ miles and $11^1/_2$ miles.

Starting points:

Parbold railway station; Pathfinder Map 699, Chorley and Burscough Bridge, map reference 491107 (or Landranger Map 108, Liverpool).

Appley Bridge railway station; Pathfinder Map 711, Wigan and Ormskirk, map reference 524094 (or Landranger Map 108, Liverpool).

(You need both Pathfinder maps for the walk)

How to get there:

By car – to Parbold on the A5209 between Wigan and Burscough. After crossing the railway and canal, turn right to the railway station, where there is a car park.

– to Appley Bridge, just south of the B5375 $1/_2$ mile south of its junction with the A5209 between Wigan and Parbold. There is a car park at the railway station, on the left before crossing railway and canal.

By train – to Parbold on the Manchester to Southport line.

– to Appley Bridge on the Manchester to Southport line.

West of Wigan attractive hills divided by the valley of the River Douglas drop down to the coastal plain and provide fine walking combined with views of the Lancashire and North Wales coasts, even to Anglesey and the Lake District on the right day. Through the valley run the Manchester-Southport railway and the Leeds and Liverpool Canal, both of which may be useful on these walks.

North of the valley the high point is Harrock Hill, with its ruined windmill, reached by a loop of 6 miles from Parbold to Appley Bridge. South of the valley is Ashurst's Beacon, reached by a loop of about $5^1/_2$

miles from Appley Bridge to Parbold, so a total walk of $11^1/_2$ miles. To walk only one of the loops, you could use the train from Parbold to Appley Bridge or vice versa, or the canal towpath. It's $2^1/_2$ miles along the towpath between Parbold and Appley Bridge, so that would produce a Harrock Hill circular of $8^1/_2$ miles or an Ashurst's Beacon circular of 8, or you could begin and end the latter circuit at Appley Bridge by walking back along the towpath from Gillibrand Bridge, which would be $5^1/_2$ miles.

But where does the title fit into all this? Well, as you approach Appley Bridge, you descend an attractive valley called Fairy Glen (although naughty gnomes deposit litter in places) and the monument on Ashurst's Beacon, erected in 1798 by Sir William Ashurst in expectation of an invasion by the French, is either a squat obelisk or an elongated pyramid!

The Walk

From the Southport-bound platform of the railway station at Parbold, go through the subway under the line. From the station car park, turn right along the main road towards the row of shops.

Beyond the shops, turn right along Tan House Lane, a road of pleasant houses, ending, on the right, with a towered convent. Cross the road ahead and ascend the fenced track between the school on the right and the pigeon loft on the left.

Climb the stile and follow the path along the left-hand hedge to leave Parbold behind. Over to the right now the monument on Ashurst's Beacon is visible above the trees. Turn left and then right as the path keeps along the edge of the wood, and the landscape is an attractive mix of open fields and groups of trees. You climb gently.

The path then takes you over a narrow wooden footbridge and a stile. From there bear right up the field, keeping just to the right of a hollow with trees round it, and the next stile will appear in the fence ahead. The spring trees were full of birdsong when I last did this walk.

Keep straight on up the field, where the line of the path is just visible, and, as you look back, the view begins to suggest that you've climbed.

Walk 7

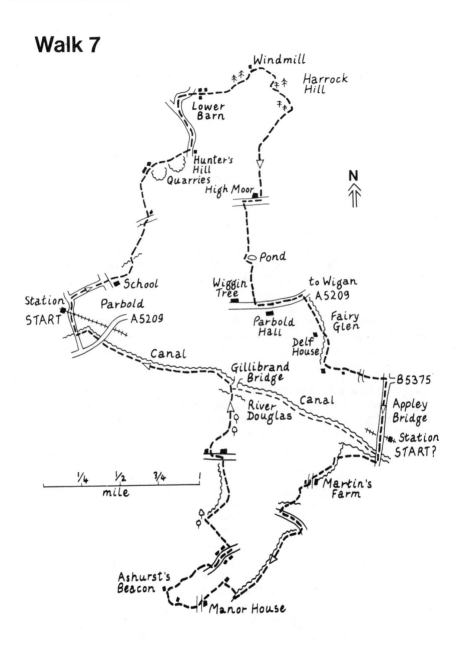

A stile beside a metal gate brings you out onto a road up which you turn right. You leave it after a few yards by a stile on the left before the house. Keep by the right-hand fence, climb a stile in a morass of mud and continue up the field ahead to the corner of the wall and along by the wall. Out to the left you can look over the flat coastal plain.

When you reach the track beyond the next stile, turn right and then bear left at the fork and up past old, stone farm buildings and a splash of golden gorse. Keep on uphill, up the sandy track round Hunter's Hill, with the quarries on the right and tremendous views on the left. Finally you squeeze between two rocks and emerge on a road.

Now my cruelty becomes apparent: turn left down the road to lose most of the height you have gained since Parbold! You descend past the house called "Hunters Meet". At the foot of the hill turn right, not up the gateposted drive to Harrock Hall but along Jacksons Lane. Where the road forks, bear right through the farm with a blossomy, daffodilly, even squirrely valley on the right. Don't you like the sign for Lower Barn Cottage?

Walk straight up the drive through Lower Barn Farm and up the concrete drive beyond. Climb the stile ahead and ascend between fences – and lambs. The stone slabs may prove useful. Follow the old sunken track, curving left as it climbs, past contorted tree-roots.

You come to a stile and continue along the top of the field with super views again and wool-strewn gorse and holly and hawthorn. At the next stile, keep to the right of the wall. Before the next fence, climb the stone step-stile on the left, and then the stile which leads into the wood.

Beyond the trees, bear left up to the remains of Harrock Hill's windmill with its views over the plain and back to Ashurst's Beacon. This is the end of your morning climb and a good spot from which to contemplate, if you are fortunate with visibility, Southport and the Lancashire coastline, and perhaps the Lake District and North Wales coast.

Return to the wall and turn left alongside it to the stile beside the metal gate. Over the stile, keep by the left-hand fence (we enjoyed the company of twin white lambs and twin black ones) towards the mast and trig. point. Are Rivington Pike and Winter Hill visible?

Turn right along by the plantation, don't bother to use the stile into the plantation, but do turn left through the gate at the end of the trees and uphill by the fence. Larks were singing like mad and eight mallard rose from a hidden pond.

" . . . the remains of Harrock Hill's windmill . . . "

Climb the stile ahead and keep on up the field to the end of the wood. Then turn right over the stile and between hedge and wood, so that you don't actually reach the trig. point. The path descends gently, and we looked to the right to see mysterious horseriders galloping up to the windmill. A pheasant coughed in Butteries Wood ahead, near which you pass on the fenced path with its escort of trees. When you reach the concrete drive from Harrock Hall, bear left up it to the road, with Ashurst's Beacon dominating the view ahead.

Turn right past the High Moor Restaurant and then, so that you can't waste your time in the pub ahead (more evidence of my cruelty), turn down the first drive on the left. Where the drive swings right, keep straight on along the muddy track. There were three muddy geese, one of which, when our backs were turned, sneaked up behind us with neck outstretched and wings spread, before retreating in the face of a flapped map. This is a use which the Ordnance Survey perhaps did not contemplate.

Pass a pond with a tree that tempts climbing with wet consequences (I restrained my wife with difficulty).

Follow the track as it bears right beside a large pond and, immediately after the pond, climb the stile on the left and keep on the path to the left. When you reach the hedge and bank, bear right beside them. Pass through the hedge, and then turn right alongside the hedge and under the wires, and down the track to the road, with the Wiggin Tree to the right and Parbold Hall to the left.

You're not interested in food, so turn left along the busy road and you have an impressive view of the Hall's asymmetrical facade. At the foot of the hill, turn right along the drive on the outside of the bend. Either keep on the drive (the right of way) or go through the gap in the fence on the left and along the narrow path through the trees beside Sprodley Brook, over which you will need to stride. At the right time of year there is a feast of bluebells here in Fairy Glen.

If you've walked along the track, then, at the end of the fence on the left, descend to the stream and go through the fence there, but do not cross the stream. If you've followed the path by the brook, go through the fence and keep on the right bank.

Remain on the right bank until you can cross the brook by the wooden footbridge below Delf House (where there were a wren and two cock pheasants), and take the path downstream between railings and above a waterfall, where a wagtail flew from rock to rock. As we ate our lunch there, a rabbit disappeared into its burrow just behind us.

You pass between further railings and descend the drive ahead to the farm gate. Do not go through it but climb the stile on the left and follow the edge of the field round the hill with the Douglas valley to your right. A kestrel showed its colours beautifully.

Go over the stile to the left of the house, beside the garden pond, and up the path on the opposite side of the drive. A couple more fields bring you to a road, you turn down it for a few yards and then, before the road bends left, you take the path on the left.

At the road junction with Skull House Lane, turn right down the road into Appley Bridge and before long you are at its railway station.

Continue downhill (or, if starting from the station, turn left down the road) past the Railway Inn with its terrace overlooking the canal. Cross the canal and then the River Douglas, and immediately beyond that take the path on the right, with a Chinese something-or-other on the far bank.

Keep along the riverbank until, near the superfluous ladder-stile, you bear left across the field to the end of the hedge, keep to the right of the hedge, and cross the bridge over the stream ahead. On the far bank, turn left along the clear path. You can look right across the valley to Parbold Hall.

When you reach the buildings of Martin's Farm, at the end of the wood and water walk, bear left to the road and up the track opposite, to the left of the stone house. The track climbs and curves and comes to a junction, where you take the sunken track to the right. Sunken means soggy, but not for long, for, after crossing a stream, it begins to climb up natural rock steps.

Arrival at a road is a shock. Turn left along it, with Fairy Glen and Appley Bridge to the left. Beyond the farmhouse turn right up the track through the trees, following another stream, with the track passing under a fallen beech and climbing steadily.

This very pleasant track disposes of most of the climbing for you. Where it turns left to a farm, turn off right down a path to the stream with a stout stile before it, and round the hillside. Negotiate the horses, climb the stile by the gate, and turn left up the drive from the farm. When you reach the road, Ashurst's Beacon is visible ahead.

Turn left up the road again (more cruelty) and, still opposite the garden wall of the Manor House, take the narrow path on the right between fence and hollies. Bear slightly right across the next field to the stile by the drive and pond. Cross the drive and follow the footpath between pond and fence. Over the stile ahead, turn right and up to the Beacon – for the enjoyment of the people of Wigan.

Look south over Skelmersdale, over Parbold, across to Harrock Hill, Appley Bridge, Gathurst, Wigan and the West Pennines. If it's a good day, you should see as far as much of the coasts of Lancashire and North Wales.

From the Beacon, bear right (eastwards) down through the trees to the fence and turn left along the track. Go over the stile beside the gate and then turn right along by the fence. Near the bottom of the field, climb the stile on the right, descend to the footbridge and, on the far bank of the stream, follow the edge of the field to the left. Drop steeply to the road and turn left down it – yes *down* it!

" . . . *turn right and up to the Beacon . . .* "

Pass Catterall's Farm and the converted barn with a pretty stream and lovely spring gardens. Opposite the drive to Bangham Farm (beyond the house called Woodlands), take the track to the left round the hillside. A flock of chaffinches kept us company along the edge of the fields. When you reach the wood, follow the track down to the right and then along by the left-hand fence. At the bottom of the field, go over the stile on the left, across to the corner of the next field, through the gateway and down by the fence with the valley on its left. The path follows the ruts downhill with a lovely view over a farm to Parbold Beacon.

Climb the gated stile before the farm and turn left along the road, but then turn right up the drive to the next house. Keep to the right of the buildings and take the right fork of the track. The track descends into a wood, showing its first celandines, wood anemones and wild garlic when we last passed through.

At the foot of the slope beyond the wood, take the right fork in the track again across the last field before the canal (or use the parallel path along the left side of the watercourse ahead). Parbold's two church spires are to the left. You recross the Douglas and arrive at the Leeds and Liverpool canal at Gillibrand Bridge. Turn right for Appley Bridge or left for Parbold (each is about $1^1/_4$ miles away).

If you have turned left, a canal milepost tells you it's $99^1/_4$ miles to Leeds on this lovely, wide, wooded, reedy section of the canal. Boaters, anglers and mallard were at play. Then houses and gardens come down to the canal and it's still very pleasant. On the outside of the canal's sharp bend to the left is a dry dock.

As you round that corner, Parbold's windmill comes into view and you climb up at the concrete bridge and turn right along the road across it back to the railway station. Look back and Ashurst's Beacon is to be seen on its hilltop. Enticing open fires burnt in narrowboats – and our feet felt warm too as we climbed up to the station platform.

The Towpath Routes

If you are walking only the northern loop and you start or finish with the stretch of canal from Appley Bridge to Parbold, turn left out of Appley Bridge station (or continue down the road past the station) and over the canal. Turn right along the towpath past Appley Locks and Hand Lane Bridge to Gillibrand Bridge (number 40) and then follow the description for the full walk.

If you are walking the southern loop and wish to return along the towpath from Gillibrand Bridge to Appley Bridge, turn right along the towpath from Gillibrand Bridge and pass Hand Lane Bridge and Appley Locks to reach the bridge at Appley Bridge, where you turn left over the canal and up the road to the station.

8. FOREST AND FOOTPRINTS

Frodsham – Weaver Navigation – Kingsley – Delamere – Manley
Common – Woodhouse Hill – Frodsham.

Distance: between 9 miles and 18 miles.

Starting points:

Frodsham railway station; Pathfinder Map 757, Ellesmere Port (East),
map reference 518778 (or Landranger Map 117, Chester and Wrexham).

Delamere railway station; Pathfinder Map 757, Ellesmere Port (East),
map reference 555704 (or Landranger Map 117, Chester and Wrexham).

How to get there:

By car – to Frodsham on the A56 between Warrington and Chester. In
the centre of Frodsham, turn left along the B5132, under the railway line
and turn left into the car park immediately beyond the Gaping Gander.

– to Delamere, turn left in Frodsham along the B5394 and then on the
B5152 via Hatchmere. Just after crossing the railway at Delamere station,
turn right to Delamere Forest Visitor Centre and park in the car park on
the right at Linmere Picnic Area.

By train – to Frodsham on the Manchester to Chester via Warrington
Bank Quay line.

– to Delamere on the Manchester to Chester via Northwich line.

This is a walk of four landscapes. You begin with the broad, sweeping
curves of the River Weaver in its green valley, and that has its hidden
delights. Then rolling Cheshire farmland, the second landscape, takes
you across fields to the third landscape, the beautiful Delamere Forest, a
lovely mixture of young trees and mature ones, of conifers and
deciduous trees, and no massed ranks of plantations are obvious. The
paths and tracks are a pleasure, and, since much of your time in the
forest is on the Sandstone Trail, the route is well waymarked with the
Trail's sign of a footprint with an S in it. We relished the smells of the
trees and the foxes, and the symphony of birdsong.

The Sandstone Trail then leads you back across farmland again to the fourth landscape, the striking sandstone edge leading from Woodhouse Hill to Beacon Hill above Frodsham, with view after view out over the Mersey estuary. That is exciting.

The complete route is a demanding 18 miles, with the toughest bit coming when you reach the sandstone climax near the end, so you might want to do the walk in sections. You could split the walk into its eastern and western legs, about 9 miles each, by using trains from Manchester to Frodsham and back from Delamere, or vice versa. A day return to Chester would allow you to use both lines. Or you could make use of the approximately 2-hourly bus service from Frodsham to Hatchmere, about a mile up the road from Delamere station.

Instead, you could do a northern circuit of $10^1/_2$ miles, following the main route from Frodsham to Kingsley, then across to Woodhouse Hill and back along the main route to Frodsham. Its southern equivalent, from Delamere via Kingswood to Kingsley and back to Delamere, is also about $10^1/_2$ miles. And even more variations are possible using that Frodsham, Kingsley and Hatchmere bus – but do check the times. Time your arrival at Kingsley right and there can be lunchtime food in front of a log fire at the Red Bull.

Try all four landscapes – or some of them – in all four seasons – or some of them – for super variety.

The Walk

From the car park in Frodsham, turn right along the road to the A56. From Frodsham station exit, turn left down to the road and right to the A56. Now turn right along the A56, which, thanks to the M56, is quite a pleasant road, cutting through the sandstone and passing the interesting and unexpected Methodist church.

The road becomes less interesting but you soon drop down to Frodsham Bridge over the River Weaver, with the railway viaduct to the left and the M56 beyond that. Do not cross the bridge but turn right along the track, from which you can admire the road bridge. The path goes through a tunnel of hedges and then onto the bank to avoid a wet patch, but quickly reverts to its hedged route.

Walk 8

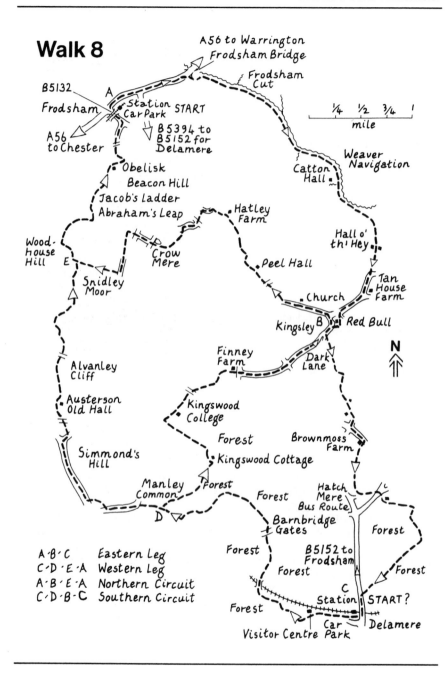

A·B·C   Eastern Leg
C·D·E·A   Western Leg
A·B·E·A   Northern Circuit
C·D·B·C   Southern Circuit

" . . . you soon drop down to Frodsham Bridge over the River Weaver . . . "

It negotiates old willow trees and then is back to the peaceful bank of the river, with the still water providing perfect reflections of the trees and two herons on my last visit. The River Weaver now comes in from the left and, from Frodsham Lock, you follow the path along the bank of the Frodsham Cut. Pass the end of the bridge leading onto the island between the Cut and the river and continue beside the Cut to the main river. Over to the right is Beacon Hill, the end of your walk.

Beyond a stile you follow the path along the edge of the river, which pursues its course in wide, sweeping curves. Larks continuously chorused overhead, lapwings cried in the field towards the extensive buildings of Bradley Orchard Farm on the right, and a boating family washed up after breakfast.

There is a rather unfriendly gate to conquer before you cross a sidestream, but do not be deterred, and keep on along the bank. The next gate was slightly more user-friendly. Now Catton Hall is to your right and the wooded hillside coming down to the riverbank on the left adds to the attractiveness of the valley.

Close to Catton Hall you cross two stiles and a bridge to get over another sidestream, and then another stile takes the path between riverside trees on the left and a hedge on the right. When I last walked this stretch of the bank, there was a feast of flowers: celandines, stitchwort, bluebells, campion, violets, wild garlic and king-cups were all in flower, foxgloves were on their way up, and in boggy patches the iris leaves were growing tall. Rooks chattered and pheasant barked, and the warm sun of spring shone through the trees. It was perfect, and I just had to stop for a coffee-break.

Here the hills on the left have receded from the river to be replaced by those on the right and wet feet are avoided by plank-bridges. Climb the stile, emerge from the trees, cross a little concrete bridge and a plank one and then turn right beyond a line of trees with a stream flowing among them. The first tree had a "No Shooting" notice on it when I was last here. A clear track takes you uphill, away from the river.

Beside the track, I found someone's discarded literary endeavours, saying 13 times, "I must come into my line when the whistle has been blown". I leave you to speculate why they were there. Further up the track, the men from North West Water had a problem: one of the three 42-inch mains carrying water from North Wales to Liverpool had burst and they were being forced to sit in the sun for 5 hours until the head of water had reduced sufficiently for the welder to start work!

As you climb the track, look back into the valley. Pass between the buildings of Hall o' th' Hey and down the drive ahead, with the village of Kingsley before you. At the road, bear right towards Kingsley, past Tan House Farm and its attractive datestone, and into the village.

Beyond Brook House on the right, at the junction with Chapel Lane on the left, turn left along the footpath which crosses the front lawn of the brick house and along the bank of the brook. At the road, turn right and immediately left to continue along the bank of the brook, with the attractive garden of the Red Bull on the right.

If you are walking the northern circuit back to Frodsham, you turn right along the road towards the pub, but otherwise turn left, not up The Hurst, but along the more main road past the butcher's. The road rises to the second junction with The Hurst and you bear left up the track just beyond, now with those walking the southern circuit. The bridleway is deeply sunken and one bank was a mass of refugee honesty flowers.

The path proceeds pleasantly between fences and along by the hedge ahead, turns right to follow the hedge, and then zigs to the right and zags to the left, and rises between hedges. Now a drive, it passes two farms and reaches a road. At the second farm, did you notice the shape of the holes in the walls at first-floor level in the barn? Are they just right for pitching bales through, do you think?

Turn right along the road, and left at the crossroads. At the far end of Brownmoss Farm, turn right through the farmyard towards School Lane and Hatchmere. After a straight stretch, your broad path bears left, still between hedge and fence, and then on towards a white house. Here we watched a heron, coming in to land, driven off by a pair of crows.

By the house, keep straight on along the drive towards Hatchmere. When the drive turns right (with Hatch Mere visible to the right, with the bus route back to Frodsham there too), take the path to the left for School Lane again. At the immediate fork, keep right to stay near the edge of the wood and continue along the drive to arrive at School Lane.

Cross into Post Office Lane and climb the stile on the right beside the first gate, with Delamere Forest ahead. Keep along by the hedge and up the track between the farm buildings, avoiding electric wires, of which there were many. Beyond the buildings, turn left along by the hedge, over the stile, and still on, to the end of the next field. Climb carefully over the remains of the stile to the left of the gateway and turn right up the sunken track, over two stiles, with the forest close ahead and the mast up on Pale Heights. I persuaded a gentle bullock to lick my finger with its rasping, grasping tongue.

Bear left downhill and then turn left along the track towards the white bungalow. The track curves right to a stile by a gate and you continue between gorse bushes and along the foot of the slope.

Over the stile, you turn right along the wooded track to enter Delamere Forest, dropping down between tall trees, a mixture of coniferous and deciduous like so much of the forest. At the T-junction of tracks, turn right, and go straight on at the crossroads of tracks. When the main track swings right, leave it for the path ahead which keeps near the edge of the forest, with, on the left, an open field containing a barn.

You glimpse a lake through the trees on the left and then reach the road, where you turn left to Delamere station (or right to Hatchmere for the occasional bus back to Frodsham). If you are walking the eastern leg and now wish to catch a train back to Manchester, turn down the steps on the right on the near side of the bridge. Otherwise cross the bridge and turn right down the steps on the far side, to be joined by those starting a walk from Delamere station, who turn right on leaving the Chester-bound platform. When I was last at the station, its buildings were being converted into a café, so it may be open by the time your mouth is.

Follow the track parallel to the line, through the car park, where car-borne walkers may join the route, and along the path to "Forest Information". The path takes you out onto the road, where you turn right. Keep on past the bridge and along to the Visitor Centre. Pop in and then continue along the road, now more roughly surfaced.

Soon there are trees on both sides and a path bears right with a Forest Trail and Soils Trail sign. That's the way you go. After only a few yards, the trees on the left end and you walk along the path with the open field on your left. The main path turns right (the Forest Trail), but you keep on along the edge of the trees to follow the Soils Trail.

The fenced alcoves are to allow you to inspect the soil in cross-section and, convenient though they may be, are not to be used for any other purpose! Your route lies between fine pines – and badger setts? With farm buildings up to your left, the path turns right, down to another soil sample, and then left to a T-junction with another path.

Turn left, cross the stream and then take the path on the right along the bank of the stream to a footbridge. Do not cross the bridge but keep on along the path and you will arrive at a broad track, the Sandstone Trail, with "footprint and S" waymark.

Turn right to cross the railway line by a substantial bridge. At the junction of tracks, keep straight on, and similarly at the crossroads, following the sign for Barnbridge Gates. Now you are between deciduous trees. As you approach the road at Barnbridge Gates, a sign points your way to Frodsham.

Cross the road and take the track opposite. At the first junction, turn left and, at the next junction, with young trees on the left, keep straight on towards the hills ahead. At the forest edge, bear left along the track. You reach a track with the mast on Pale Heights to the left, and you there turn right down to a forest road, but do not let it lead you uphill.

Instead, turn back left along it until it swings left. You there leave it for the path ahead.

At the crossroads, keep nearly straight on to descend a deeply-sunken track and cross the stream which tinkles delightfully beneath the track. Then turn up the next track on the right, signposted to Manley Common. The sun came out and dappled the trees beautifully.

Soon you reach the edge of the forest. For the main route continue through the stile and along the track by the edge of the field with Simmond's Hill ahead of you (but to walk the southern circuit to return to Delamere, turn right along the path through the forest). At the houses of Manley Common, turn left along the road, with good views of hills to the left.

When the road bends left after Stonehouse Farm, climb the stile on the right, go up to the corner of the field, and left over the stile beside the gate. Keep along the edge of the field beside the magnificent holly hedge, heed the warning, cross the road, and turn right.

Pass church and school and viewpoint-layby, and, at the foot of the hill, turn up the road on the right. Opposite the gate to Simmonds Hill, climb the stile on the left and follow the path along by the hedge and then leftwards across the field. Cross the lane and keep along the left side of the field to the stile and beyond it turn right, to pass below the old house on a new site – Austerson Old Hall transported from Nantwich.

Turn right to keep along the edge of the Hall's grounds and left along the foot of Alvanley Cliffs. We sat with our backs to the old stone bank and looked out across a vivid yellow foreground to refinery and power station as we took a break and listened to a hoarse pheasant.

As you continue, an expansive view across the Mersey appears to the right of Helsby Hill and the hills of the walk's end are to be seen. Follow the path round the edge of the wood and down to the stile, across the road, and over the stile on the far side. The path descends a gully along the field-side (lots of rabbits were scampering into the briar patch on the left at our approach), climbs a stile and steps, and keeps along the field edge to the next stile.

There follow the path round to the right, over the footbridge into Queen Charlotte's Wood, and along through the trees to the left. Turn up the steps on the right to stay inside the wood and emerge on a road, at a caravan site. Then it's left down the road for 100 yards before turning back right along the track.

The track climbs gently, and that is fortunate as the miles may be beginning to tell among the birches of Snidley Moor. Keep on the main path, observing the Sandstone Trail waymarks. Turn left at the fence on the edge of the wood, with the back of Beacon Hill ahead of you, and you are joined by those walking the northern circuit. At the next fork, keep right along by the edge of the wood, and right again, still along the edge of the wood.

But do follow the path when it curves to the left (at a field corner) beside a stone wall to cross Woodhouse Hill with its Iron Age fort. The path then brings you to the edge of the hills, with traffic noise rising from the plain ahead, and you descend the hillside, bearing right to slabs of rock at a vantage point among the trees. From there you look out to Helsby Hill, to power station and oil refinery, and across the M56 to the Mersey and Liverpool. Wow!

Keep to the right, through the trees and round the hillside. Below me on a crag a hidden climber clinked. The path is level along the top of the wood and swings to the right as it approaches Dunsdale Hollow, with views down into the Hollow and over the Mersey again. Then it drops down a rock staircase, called "Abraham's Leap" but no leaping is necessary. The path then swings round to the left along the cliff-side with more views down-river. It crosses an area of very red soil, and arrives at the foot of Jacob's Ladder, a very steep, very red and very rocky stairway to the skies.

That route probably involves long legs or scuffed knees. You may prefer to follow the Sandstone Trail waymarks to the right and back up the steps, with the message "Not so far now", and along the top of Jacob's Ladder.

Back on the clifftop, you reach a stile where the Sandstone Trail leaves the wood and crosses the golf course. Here you part company with the Sandstone Trail and keep along the path at the top of the wood. Whenever the path divides, keep to the upper one and you should stay beside the golf course, with a succession of great views. The war memorial obelisk appears ahead and that's what you're making for.

Keep to the top path, but do not follow it up the stone steps and through the wall into the grounds of the Forest Hills Leisure Complex. Instead you have to scramble down to the next path. It's a little undignified, but the only way I could ensure that you didn't miss the path up to the hilltop climax of the walk. Again keep to the upper path at any fork and you ought to arrive on the flat top of the cliff with the war memorial not far ahead.

A helpful toposcope will describe the view, which is tremendous. I can't claim ever to have seen Snowdon, but, if it's a clear day, you should see as far as my home hill of Winter Hill, near Bolton, 25 miles away, also Stanlow oil refinery, the Liverpool cathedrals, Widnes/Runcorn bridge, and the power stations at Bromborough, Bold and Fiddler's Ferry.

" . . . the view, which is tremendous . . . " – Beacon Hill, Frodsham

After having your fill of the view – or perhaps because your train is due – cross to the far side of the war memorial, from where you can see the start of this walk at Frodsham. Just beyond, your path descends the hillside to the right, turns to the left, left again on meeting another path, then back to the right. Keep on that path down to the right until you reach the houses.

Then descend the asphalt drive back to the left. It narrows into a path and, where it forks, go right. Descend steps to a drive, turn right to the road, right up the road, left through the first gateway, and along the path ahead.

At the next footpath, turn left, and then right down the first road, Kingsway. At the end of the road, turn left and the car park entrance and the station are not far ahead on the right. From them you can look up to the obelisk on the hill above you, and it's probably then that you discover you must have left your camera up there after taking pictures of the view . . .

Kingsley to Woodhouse Hill

When you reach the road by the Red Bull in Kingsley, for Frodsham turn right and follow the road round to the left, back to the right and left along the main road, past school and church. Not far beyond the church, climb the sandstone steps on the right, negotiate the holly bush, and then bear left along by the right-hand hedge, with views to the right beyond the Weaver. At the end of the field, continue by the right-hand fence and hedge and over the stile to the drive and road.

A few paces to the right down the road, turn left over a stile and descend the path which bears left to cross the stream by a footbridge and climb up to a fenced track. Turn right up it and in the open field again keep along by the right-hand hedge, past the interesting buildings of Peel Hall, with moat, and left along its drive.

At the T-junction of tracks, climb the stile beside the gate ahead, and keep along the stony track first on the left side of the field and then bearing right across it. In the next field, keep to the left again and Frodsham Beacon will appear to your left. Over the stile at the end of the long field, turn left along the drive from Hatley Farm (with carpets to protect the drive from cows' dirty feet!).

You join a road and continue ahead to where a footpath crosses the road. Go through the gateway or over the stile on the left and up the field to the gate, beside which is a stile letting you out onto the main road. Turn left and then up the minor road on the right, following it uphill, past two roads on the right.

A little way uphill is fenced land on the left, belonging to Frodsham Parish Council, where there are to be "No Unauthorised Activities" –

whatever they are. There turn left towards the gate and left over the stile. Now follow the path round to the right, searching diligently for any unauthorised activities which may be taking place among the brambles and bracken. The broad, hedged path, which feels like an old one, shows you the back of Frodsham Beacon to the right and takes you past Crow Mere to a crossroads, where you keep straight on.

At the T-junction, climb the stile on the far side of the road and keep along by the fence, with magnificent pampas grass on the left. To the right and then ahead are extensive Mersey views. When you reach the bottom of the field, go over the stile and left along the path, with the Sandstone Ridge now to your right. Cross the sunken lane and, beyond the ladder-stile, bear slightly left to the stile not much before the end of the field.

Turn right along the road to the bend and there turn right along the track signposted to Woodhouse Hill. The track becomes a path, descends into a wood, and keeps on downhill. As it begins to climb, it meets the Sandstone Trail coming in from the left, and so, now on the route of the full walk, you follow the Sandstone Trail waymarks.

Manley Common to Kingsley

When you reach the edge of the forest, do not leave it for the houses of Manley Common but turn right along the broad path. This keeps the edge of the forest in sight on the left until it crosses the second small stream. Then it keeps straight on, bears left at a junction with a track and follows the track to a T-junction of tracks. Turn left, and left again at the T-junction with the stone-surfaced track.

At the next junction, turn left to leave the cycle trail and pass Kingswood Cottage. Just beyond it, the main track bends right, but you take the path ahead. After 100 yards or so, it forks and you turn left. The path now has the remains of a wire fence on the right and then filter beds on the left as you reach the edge of the forest and follow it. Along this path I was a little surprised to find myself at the tail-end (literally) of a convoy of eight bullocks.

You arrive at a stile with an informative set of signposts and turn right into the wood along a narrow path, making for Kingsley. I disturbed a squirrel as I approached Kingswood College. After only a short strip of woodland, climb the stile ahead and keep along the right-hand boundary for two fields. In the third field you keep straight on up the field, aiming just to the left of an electricity pylon.

Cross the road, go through the gap in the hedge opposite, and bear half-right across the field to the stile in the hedge, with wide views ahead. I decided against gleaning the remains of the potato crop as I crossed the field. Beyond that stile, aim to the right for the downhill corner of the field to find the stile on the left just before the corner.

Another stile lurks in the hedge ahead and, over that, you turn left alongside the hedge, over the next stile and up to the farm drive. (The route is waymarked but, in those last two fields, different from that shown on the O.S. map.) You reach the drive by an attractive but uninformative footpath sign.

Turn right along the drive and, at the road junction by Finney Farm, keep straight on. At the next crossroads, again keep on up Dark Lane, which, as it descends into Kingsley, becomes narrow and pretty. There is a thatched cottage to delight the eye and a well-weathered bust of the bard stands outside Shakespeare Cottage. At the road junction, turn right for a few yards and then left up the track just past the end of The Hurst, with those doing the full walk.

9. FOLLY AND FANTASY

Congleton –·Congleton Edge – Mow Cop – Little Moreton Hall –
Macclesfield Canal – Congleton.

Distance: between 9 miles and $12^1/_2$ miles

Starting point:

Congleton railway station; Pathfinder Map 776, Congleton, map
reference 872623 (or Landranger Map 118, Stoke-on-Trent and Macclesfield). (You will need Pathfinder Map 792, Kidsgrove and Leek, too for
this walk.)

How to get there:

By car – to Congleton on the A34 south of Wilmslow and from the town
centre take the A527 (towards Biddulph) to the railway station, where
there is a car park (with charge).

By train – to Congleton on the Manchester to Stoke-on-Trent line.

You can almost fall from the platform at Congleton station onto the
towpath of the Macclesfield Canal to begin the most southerly of the
walks in this book. The towpath takes you to an old railway line now
converted into a path. You then ascend to a glorious wooded ridge
which leads you southwards, with views all around, to the folly of Mow
Cop Castle, 1000 feet above the sea. It was erected in about 1750 by
Randle Wilbraham of Rode Hall as an eye-catcher and is famous as the
site of an open-air meeting in 1807 which led to the formation of the
Primitive Methodist denomination. In celebration of the centenary of that
meeting, 70,000 people worshipped here in one day.

From there you drop down through woods to the plain and then decide
whether you wish to return directly to the canal for the shorter walk of 9
miles.

For the longer route, more woodland walking and a handsome house
take you to the canal, where again you have a decision to make: should
you return directly to Congleton for a walk of $10^1/_2$ miles or make a
diversion to Little Moreton Hall, a further 2 miles in all, to see that star

of a million calendars, perhaps the most romantic and fantastic half-timbered house in the country? Do go inside if you can, to see the amazing bay-windows in the courtyard and the interior of the long gallery precariously perched on the top of the house – and to sample the refreshments, maybe. (If you wish to check whether the house will be open, telephone Congleton 272018.) Then all routes lead along the quiet and level towpath back to Congleton.

On the April day when I last did this walk, I was particularly fortunate with the weather, for a light fall of snow overnight, which whitened the Peak District and dappled my path, gave way to a day of brilliant clarity, perfect for views of distant hills, and rolled-up shirtsleeves warmth when I had left the heights of the outward walk. That's the best sort of day for this walk, but almost any day should bring you enjoyment.

The Walk

From the station car park turn left over the bridge across the line with Bosley Cloud ahead to the left and Congleton Edge ahead to the right. Once across the bridge, turn back to the right past the Railway Hotel and go under the road bridge on the right and down onto the canal towpath. Or, from the Stoke-bound platform, go out through the gate, under the road and back to the left down onto the towpath.

You make a very quick getaway from the town as a straight stretch of canal takes you eastwards, past a mass of blackthorn blossom. Beyond a handsome milestone showing 21 miles to Marple at the northern end of the canal, the houses end and the canal swings left with Bosley Cloud up ahead and a railway viaduct to your left.

The canal is on a high embankment over Dane in Shaw Brook. Your ridge route to Mow Cop can be seen back to the right. Just beyond the aqueduct over the old railway is an interesting dock, but you leave the canal by the stile immediately before the aqueduct, descend the steps to the old line, and turn right along it. Notice that the canal bridge is of stone but the water is in a cast-iron trough.

This old railway to Biddulph, now a trail, is well-wooded and provides excellent level walking. Keep left of the fence and bank if you wish to avoid any horses. Your ridge comes into view again as you curve round to the right.

Walk 9

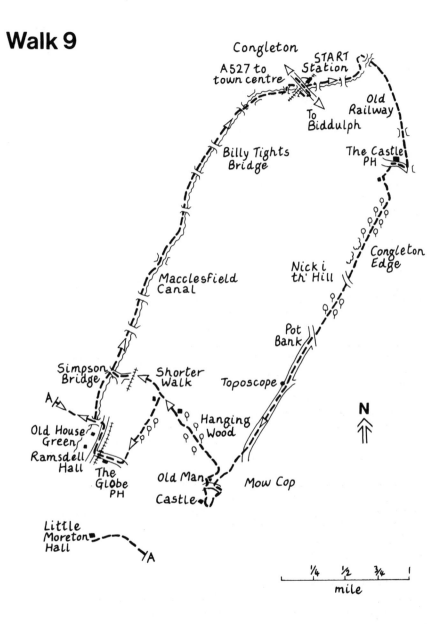

Congleton

A527 to town centre

START Station

To Biddulph

Old Railway

Billy Tights Bridge

The Castle PH

Macclesfield Canal

Nick i th' Hill

Congleton Edge

Pot Bank

Simpson Bridge

Shorter Walk

Toposcope

Old House Green

Hanging Wood

Ramsdell Hall

The Globe PH

Old Man Castle

Mow Cop

Little Moreton Hall

N

¼ ½ ¾ 1
mile

Below you on the right is an old mill on the edge of Dane in Shaw. You cross a metal bridge over a road and do not descend the steps to it. Continue along the old line and you will soon see that you are nearing the start of your ridge walk.

So, at the next road, descend the steps on the right and turn right along the road past the garage and The Castle pub (yes, *past* The Castle – it's far too early in the walk to stop). On the left-hand side of the road, just beyond the pub, look out for the path climbing to the left between hedges and turn up it to start the sweaty part of the walk.

The narrow path takes you over an awkward stile and then you follow the left-hand hedge. Keep by that hedge as the path enters a valley and swings left with a house to the right, and over a stile. The clear path takes you across the remains of a wall and then up to the left and over another stile with Congleton and Jodrell Bank telescope behind you.

Still keep along the left side of the field and then steeply up to the footpath sign on the skyline. From there I could see that the hills above Macclesfield were snow-covered.

Through the stile, turn right along by the fence now that you are on Congleton Edge, and let the brisk wind cool you down as you proceed, over the next stile and along the main path through the trees. After the climb to the ridge I shall permit you to use one of the rocky hollows as a sheltered spot for a break.

The path is delightful as it wends its way along the ridge and between the stunted birches. You can look down on the railway viaduct you saw earlier and look to the left over Gillow Heath and Biddulph. The path itself is a treat of heather and bilberry, bracken and rock, and provides a continuous vista of the Cheshire plain stretching out towards the Welsh hills.

The ridge climbs gently, dips slightly, and then levels off, and ascending the ridge before you can be seen the road leading up to Mow Cop. Below to your right are pleasant farmhouses. Take care along the edge of the old quarry, so as not to make an uncontrolled descent there (or you may end your journey in the little graveyard not far ahead on the right). Descend the ridge path to the road at aptly-named Nick i th' Hill.

Cross the road and go up the sandy track opposite, which climbs back onto the ridge. The night's snow-clouds had now cleared enough to enable me to see back to Winter Hill, my "home" hill near Bolton, and in the field to my left a learner sheepdog was receiving a driving-lesson (driving sheep, that is).

One of the birches overhead had on it growths known as witches' brooms. Mingled sand-crystals and snow-crystals sparkled in the now-bright sun as I walked the edge of another quarry, and ahead to the left were coalmines in the Potteries.

Sadly you descend to a road-junction at Pot Bank, as that fine stretch of footpath is now over. Take the right-hand road ahead to remain on the ridge. I'm sorry it's road-walking for the next mile, but I've never been bothered by excessive traffic along here, and surely the view compensates. And that view is displayed on the toposcope and the excellent information board by the road-junction at Cheshire's Close, although they don't mention Winter Hill, which was clearly visible 35 miles away. To the north the hills of the Peak District were snow-capped and below me a toy train headed for Manchester.

Keep on up the road towards the distant and unobtrusive industry of North Staffordshire and then, when the road bears left away from the ridge, bear right up the track, between houses, which heads uphill towards the radio mast. Stick to the main track, past Daisy Bank Farm, with the mast now on your right, straight on at the crossroads of tracks and past the next mast to the road, with Mow Cop Castle just ahead.

Turn left down the road as far as the first house on the left and there take the footpath opposite, round the hillside. Climb up to the dramatically-placed folly. They must have been watching me at Jodrell Bank as the dish was tilted in my direction as I looked out of one of the round windows of the tower. It is an impressive rocky spot with tremendous views.

From the Castle, descend the steps to the little roundabout at the junction of tracks and bear left along the rising track. As you reach the road, the folly is impressive behind you. Turn right, up the road, for about 20 paces and then turn left along the signposted footpath. Follow the track and take the path off it to the right, and towering above you will be the Old Man of Mow, a great rock. Continue past the Old Man – Congleton and its Edge appear ahead – and keep on along the track towards the mast. Where the track turns right after the house, you turn left down the path beside fence and wall to begin your descent to the plain, some 600 feet below. At first, the path aims for the telescope.

" . . . climb up to the dramatically-placed folly . . . " – Mow Cop Castle

As you descend, across to the right is the line of the ridge you ascended, leading to Bosley Cloud and the radio tower on Sutton Common. Down below is Congleton, and to the north the hills above Macclesfield and Stockport lead round to those along the north side of Greater Manchester and west of Wigan.

The path takes you down into Hanging Wood, presumably named for its position on the hillside rather than grim associations. You'll enjoy the descent in the shelter of trees, patterned with dark splashes of holly. Agitated branches betrayed the presence of a squirrel.

When it reaches a wall, the path turns left, goes through a stile, and leaves the wood. It goes out across the field for a short distance but then turns right to keep parallel to the edge of the wood. Then it keeps to the left of the fence round a farm of many ducks.

Down to the left are the buildings of Old House Green and, farther away, Little Moreton Hall. The clear path continues downhill to a wicket-gate beside a field-gate and you bear left down the drive.

At the junction of drives, those who are doing the shorter walk continue downhill and those doing the longer walk go over the stile on the left. Those doing the longer walk, having climbed the stile, keep near the right-hand hedge and fence, with the farm buildings on the right, over the stile ahead, and still by the right-hand hedge. Then stride over the stream and stile and into the wood.

The wet path stays just inside the wood, makes you perform strange manoeuvres round a holly bush, and eventually returns you to an open field, where you again keep by the right-hand hedge.

At the end of the field, go up the drive to the road and turn right down the road, past the Globe Inn. You probably have earned a drink by now, but it looked firmly shut the lunchtime I passed. Cross the railway and you will arrive at the imposing entrance to Ramsdell Hall. It is a fine view through the gateway to the tall brick mansion.

You're only a walker, so you don't march up the drive. You turn right along the road, below the raucous rooks, and with good views of Old House Green to the left, Mow Cop Castle far right and the railway near right. After the buildings of Old House Green, go over the stile beside the field-gate on the left and along the track to the bridge over the canal.

Cross the bridge and, if you don't want to visit Little Moreton Hall, turn left, over the stile and left again along the towpath under the bridge.

To visit Little Moreton Hall, continue along the track ahead. It bears left to a stile by a gateway and then keeps to the right-hand edge of the field. You can look back to the red brick of Ramsdell Hall and ahead the amazing black and white fantasy of Little Moreton Hall begins to materialise. At the end of the long field, keep on over the stile and after the next stile bear left, diagonally across the field to the stile in the corner.

Over that stile, keep on, and the magic of Little Moreton will be wonderfully revealed to you across its goldfish-filled moat. The classic view of its intricate, lilting and tilting exterior is yours even if the house isn't open, and you won't begrudge a single yard of that extra 2 miles. I sat by the water, admired the Hall's never-still reflection, and looked up at Mow Cop Castle before retracing my steps to the canal. I hope you've remembered the way you came – but it is waymarked.

" . . . the magic of Little Moreton will be wonderfully revealed to you across its goldfish-filled moat . . . "

Back at the canal, turn left along the towpath and under the bridge for the return to Congleton. The next bridge is Simpson Bridge, where those doing the shorter circuit rejoin the longer route. The way ahead is now straightforward, pleasant and peaceful (apart from banging bird-scarers and the occasional train) and provides views of the outward, ridge walk marching with you towards Congleton.

The milestone suggests it's less than 3 miles to Congleton, and beside it I disturbed a heron, but its fishing would have been ruined by the approaching narrowboat anyway. Stone bridge succeeds stone bridge and quarter-milestones come and go. The handsome, spired church at Astbury appears to the left, with the telescope on the skyline behind it, and Bosley Cloud is ahead to the right. A little wood beside the towpath might tempt a rest.

Golfers were taking their misguided walks on both sides of the canal as I approached the footbridge with the intriguing name of Billy Tights Bridge. The golf course marks the onset of civilisation and the approaching end of the walk.

But before that you cross the roving bridge, the Macclesfield Canal's elegant solution to the problem of getting a canal horse across the canal without untying the towrope from the narrowboat. Don't be too disorientated by now walking on the opposite bank, cross the cast-iron aqueduct with the radio tower up ahead, and then cross the next roving bridge (to become even more disorientated?).

Go under the railway and the old and new road bridges and climb back up to the left to the railway station, where the platform for Manchester provides a super view of Bosley Cloud, your target for another day, perhaps.

The Shorter Walk

For the shorter walk, continue down the farm drive to the railway, cross with considerable care, and keep on to the main road. Mow Cop Castle and the Old Man of Mow are visible behind. Turn right along the road for 100 yards, cross the canal at Simpson Bridge and immediately descend to the towpath and turn left, rejoining the main route.

10. ANTLERS AND AQUEDUCTS

Marple – Macclesfield Canal – Lyme Park – Disley – Peak Forest Canal – Marple.

Distance: between 4 miles and $19^1/_2$ miles.

Starting points:

Marple railway station; Pathfinder Map 741, Stockport (South), map reference 963893 (or Landranger Map 109, Manchester).

Buxton Road/Windlehurst Road junction, High Lane; Pathfinder Map 741, Stockport (South), map reference 949854 (or Landranger Map 109, Manchester).

Disley railway station; Pathfinder Map 741, Stockport (South), map reference 973845 (or Landranger Map 109, Manchester).

(Just a few yards of the walk are on Pathfinder Map 724, Manchester and Ashton-under-Lyne, but there is no point is buying it specially.)

How to get there:

By car – to Marple railway station on the A626 between Stockport and Glossop just east of its junction with the B6102 (there is a car park at the station).

– to Disley railway station on the A6 just west of the centre of Disley between Hazel Grove and Whaley Bridge (there is a car park at the station).

By car and bus – to walk from High Lane back to your car at Marple, go by car to Marple railway station. Walk the first part of the route to the bridge with the horse-tunnel, turn right into the centre of Marple, catch the bus to the junction of Buxton Road and Windlehurst Road at High Lane, and then walk the short distance along the A6 towards Buxton until you reach the canal.

– to walk from Disley back to your car at Marple, do as set out above and then catch a bus from High Lane to Disley railway station.

– to walk from High Lane to Disley, drive to Disley railway station, catch a bus to the junction of Buxton Road and Windlehurst Road at High Lane, and then walk the short distance back along the A6 to the canal.

By train – to Marple on the Manchester to New Mills Central line.

– to Disley on the Manchester to Buxton line.

By train and bus – to start the walk from High Lane, go by train to Disley, then by bus to the junction of Buxton Road and Windlehurst Road at High Lane and walk the short distance back along the A6 to the canal.

Take delightful stretches of two canals – with aqueducts – and a fine house and park in between – with a good chance of seeing deer with antlers – and you've got a super walk.

You begin with the Marple flight of locks, taking the Peak Forest Canal 200 feet up towards the Peak District. The flight was completed in 1804 and in 1831 was joined by the Macclesfield Canal. This takes you south along the edge of the Peak District until you leave the towpath for Lyme Park, a lovely landscape containing magnificent Lyme Hall, with equally magnificent afternoon teas. You then rejoin the Peak Forest Canal which takes you north along the side of the Goyt valley back to Marple.

That main walk is 13 miles but there are some extras if you'd like them: Bowstones Loop, an additional $2^1/_2$ miles, will take you high above Lyme Park for panoramic views; the Roman Lakes Loop, which adds a mile, takes you down by the Goyt for a valley-variant to the towpath; the Aqueduct Loop descends the whole flight of 16 locks at Marple and onto the dramatic Marple Aqueduct (2 miles); and the River Goyt Loop of another mile draws you beneath the aqueduct and its companion railway viaduct. Do all the extras and you'll walk $19^1/_2$ miles.

As the temperature was in the 90s when I last did parts of this walk, I didn't feel like walking $19^1/_2$ miles and was conscious of the presence of every bit of shade and the need for shorter variations. You can reduce the walks by 3 miles by catching the bus from Marple to High Lane. Or you could split the walk at Disley (Marple to Disley 9 miles and Disley to Marple 4 miles plus relevant loops); trains are convenient for this, but buses less so if you have to return to your car. Thus Marple to Disley via the Bowstones would be $11^1/_2$ miles and Disley to Marple with the three loops would be 8 miles, both satisfying walks. Again, you could omit much of the canal walking to start from High Lane and walk to Disley (linked by bus), $8^1/_2$ miles including the Bowstones.

The walk was lovely in the lushness of high summer and would be equally good on a frosty, winter day when you need to stride along the towpaths. So please don't say this walk lacks variety or variations; it's a tremendous triangle of treats.

The Walk

From the barrier or car park at Marple station, climb the steps to the road and turn right over the line, past the strangely-shaped house to the bridge over the Peak Forest Canal. On the far side of the bridge, turn left along the towpath, passing the well-restored warehouse built by Samuel Oldknow, who ran Marple at the end of the 18th century. You climb

" . . . *you climb beside deep and narrow locks* . . . " – *Marple*

Walk 10

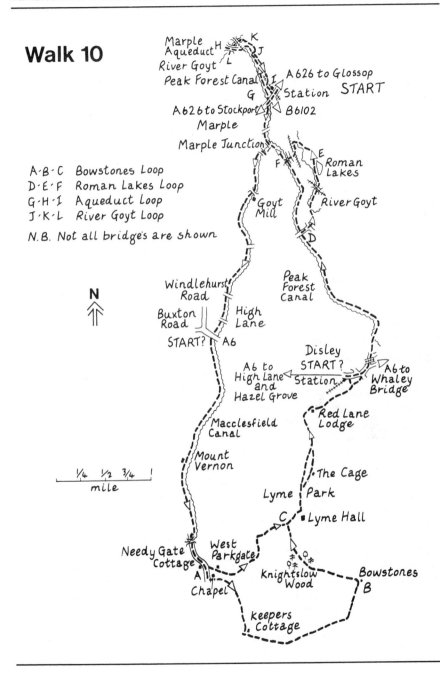

Marple Aqueduct
River Goyt
Peak Forest Canal
A626 to Glossop
Station   START
A626 to Stockport
B6102
Marple
Marple Junction
Roman Lakes

A·B·C   Bowstones Loop
D·E·F   Roman Lakes Loop
G·H·I   Aqueduct Loop
J·K·L   River Goyt Loop

N.B. Not all bridges are shown

Goyt Mill
River Goyt

N

Windlehurst Road
Peak Forest Canal
Buxton Road
High Lane
START? A6

Disley
START?
A6 to High Lane and Hazel Grove
Station
A6 to Whaley Bridge

Red Lane Lodge

¼ ½ ¾ 1
mile

Macclesfield Canal

Mount Vernon

The Cage

Lyme Park

C   Lyme Hall

Needy Gate Cottage
West Parkgate
Knightslow Wood
Bowstones
B

A
Chapel

keepers Cottage

beside deep and narrow locks with their series of stone bridges. It's a delightful start to the walk.

At the road, turn right if you want a bus to High Lane. Otherwise, mind your head as you go through the horse-tunnel and continue up the flight of locks with attendant ducks and, off to the left, large pounds. You are soon at Marple Junction, where the Macclesfield Canal meets the Peak Forest Canal. You cross the bridge and turn right along the towpath of the Macclesfield but will return to the Peak Forest later.

The towpath takes you past a warehouse and a basin, with moored narrowboats. Then wind your way up and over the roving-bridge to join the towpath on the other bank of the canal. You are now on a long level stretch of the canal at a height of 510 feet above sea-level and to the right you can look between the rooftops and out across Greater Manchester. There are boats and houses and ducks in profusion until you reach dominant Goyt Mill. Then the surroundings become increasingly rural, with Greater Manchester stretching out into the distance on the right.

The canal curves left to reveal Peak District hills ahead – and a blond horse with a beautifully-plaited tail crossed Bridge 5. Beyond it is a handsome milestone. Where there is a high wire fence on the opposite bank, look out for deer near Windlehurst Hall. They looked marvellous as they lay under the trees or made for shade, proud with their antlers. At the next bridge, we crossed the canal and took a refreshment break sitting on the steps down to the footpath so that we could watch the deer – at least 60 – peacefully grazing whilst we peacefully grazed.

Then we returned to the towpath and continued southwards, under the trees. At the next bridge (with a modern footbridge on its far side), you are in the settlement of High Lane with houses on both sides of the canal. It is still pleasant and in places gardens spill onto the towpath. High Lane continues beyond Bridge 10, as do you.

Bridge 11, beside the Bull's Head (where those starting the walk from High Lane turn right along the towpath), is a long and interestingly-shaped arch, and through it you keep on along the towpath. Not far beyond, you cross the elegant stone bridge over the High Lane arm of the canal with its moorings.

As you emerge from the green cutting and join the canal-side track, the Peak District hills seem much closer. A train could be heard hurtling down from Buxton and going under the canal, whilst another train climbed up from the opposite direction. As you cross the embankment, The Cage in Lyme Park is ahead to your left, just below the skyline. Do not follow the track over the bridge but turn left through stile or gate to keep on along the towpath. Pass the sign to Princes Incline (which led to collieries) and Middlewood Way (a super footpath along an old railway line). The Cage now appears on the skyline to the left.

Beyond the extensive marina with its multitude of boats you cross another arm of the canal at Mount Vernon and there is a useful explanation of its former busyness on the bridge ahead. The hills are much closer as you pass under the metal footbridge. Then, amidst more greenness, the canal widens, becoming river-like in the irregularity of the far bank, and turns right. Here you leave the canal and descend the long flight of stone steps on the right to reach the road.

Turn left along the road, through the tunnel under the canal and gently uphill along the pleasant road to Needy Gate Cottage. Continue up the road if you are intent on visiting the Bowstones but, if not, just beyond the cottage go through the stile on the left across the field at Green Close Farm. At the drive, turn left over the bridge and then right, at West Parkgate, into Lyme Park.

Follow the drive up through the valley, beneath the trees, beside the stream, and below clumps of rhododendrons. Go through the gate ahead (Knott Gate) into the deer park and then along the more civilised drive as it curves right and then left. As you round the hill called Knott, there are views left over Greater Manchester again. Keep down the drive, past trees for lunching under, until, with Lyme Hall in sight, there is a Gritstone Way sign on the right. Here those who have walked the Bowstones Loop rejoin the main walk. Bear left across the grass to the wooden café.

Keep the café on your right and, beyond it, turn up to the right to the entrance to the front court of the Hall. Opposite the gateway, turn left along the avenue of trees, an old, grassy drive free of vehicles, except that there were rides in a pony-cart for a short distance when we were last there. If you feel like ascending to The Cage, take the obvious path which bears right but otherwise just continue along the drive.

The Cage is hardly a thing of beauty but it does give good views across to Kinder Scout and the Downfall. From it, take the path which continues along the ridge to the left (with reservoirs to the right as you descend) to the old drive again. Continue along that drive to the modern drive (you'll see a path that cuts off the corner) and then turn right along the drive.

At the crossroads of drives by the map of Lyme Park, turn right through the gate by Red Lane Lodge. Now make your way along the lane ahead, which becomes increasingly civilised. Where it forks, bear left by the post-box. At the next corner, if you are wishing to catch the train from Disley or the bus to High Lane and thence to Marple, go through the wicket-gate on the left and down the stepped path to the station. You're even on the right platform for Manchester. For the bus you've a few more yards to go, up the path over the tunnel-mouth to the road.

If you don't need the path to the station, continue down the road and not through the wicket-gate, but past the parish church's lychgate to the road junction by the Rams Head in Disley. If you are starting the walk from Disley, from the station turn right along the main road to that junction.

From the Rams Head junction, with its fountain, follow the A6 towards Buxton and then bear left down Hollinwood Road, the first road on the left. It rapidly takes you away from the noise of the A6 and under the railway line, but do look at the fine datestone on the last cottage on the right before the bridge. Beyond the bridge, keep straight on along Hagg Bank Lane, not down to the right.

You pass Hagg Bank Farm and the Goyt valley is spread out before you, Kinder Scout on the skyline to the right. The Peak Forest Canal appears down to your right and, opposite the little wooden house of "Sunnyside", you bear right down the track and over the swing-bridge to the towpath.

Turn left along the towpath, a place of peace, moored boats, horses swishing their tails to keep the flies at bay, and welcome shade from high hedges on that very hot day when I was last here. There were trees as well as the hedges, purple loosestrife, meadowsweet, great willow-herb and occasional glimpses up the Goyt valley to New Mills. Yes, a place of peace, confirmed a moored narrowboater, until a farmer spread muck on a nearby field and flies for miles around gathered for a feast. I hurried on.

Soon the canal opens out and there are views across the valley to the hills above Strines. You pass a lift-bridge and now you can look down the Goyt valley. The house and garden at Littlewoodend looked lovely at the next bridge, under which you pass to enter a wooded stretch with birdsong, tall rushes and a breeze.

In another belt of woodland, a track creeps under the canal. You pass another lift-bridge and then, as you look ahead to the houses of Marple Bridge, there are some fine trees on the right including copper beech and sweet chestnut. Just before the next bridge was a narrowboat in Cadbury's livery, not converted into a pleasure-boat and looking rather handsome. The old cottage's garden looked gorgeous at the height of its summer fullness.

At this bridge you need to decide whether to continue along the canal or descend to Roman Lakes. For the shorter route to Marple, just keep on the towpath along a pleasant stretch of waterway, rural on the left but you will be conscious of the nearness of houses and road on the right. At red-brick Bridge 19, where those who went to Roman Lakes rejoin the canal, turn back to the right after you've been under the bridge, cross it, and follow the towpath to the right on the far bank. You are soon back at the junction of the Peak Forest and Macclesfield Canals. So cross the bridge over the Macclesfield and follow the canal down the Marple flight of locks, past the converted warehouse to the next bridge where, unless you are wishing to walk the Aqueduct Loop and possibly the River Goyt Loop, you turn right down the road back to Marple railway station.

Bowstones Loop

Past Needy Gate Cottage, continue up the road to the Methodist church and turn left up the drive immediately beyond it. Keep straight on between the two houses and to the left of the third, and then go over and through the stile by the gate. Now follow the path along the left side of the field. At the fork by the old shed, bear left and stay by the left-hand wall as you ascend. There are views back over the Cheshire plain.

You are following the edge of Lyme Park with a stone building to the left above the clough of Cluse Hay. Bowstones Farm is ahead to the left. You keep to the right-hand side of a valley, cross its stream, and then climb on its left. I thought I could just glimpse Winter Hill beyond Greater Manchester. The path is broad and clear as it leads across the field with Moorside Farm to the left, and the view back may be broad and clear too, with the canal below you. The Cage appears to the left.

The path takes you across a soggy stretch and up to a step-stile in the top right-hand corner of the field. Turn right along the drive from the farm and past Keeper's Cottage. All the tower blocks in Greater Manchester were laid out on the plain, with Winter Hill and Rivington Pike now clearly visible to the north-west, and Jodrell Bank telescope was beyond Alderley Edge.

At the far end of the garden wall round Keeper's Cottage, turn up to the left. Plod upwards beside the wall, keep looking back, and you'll arrive at a stile to see you're nearly as high as Bowstones Farm. Over to the right is the point of Shutlingsloe and on the skyline is the Windgather ridge. Bear left across the field to keep by the wall again into about four dips and up the other side, with the Post Office tower on Sutton Common to the right. To the left The Cage is below you but Lyme Hall is hidden.

You eventually reach the track along the crest of the ridge. Windgather Rocks are just on the skyline and Whaley Bridge is down in the valley. Kinder Scout is on the skyline to the left, with the Downfall obvious.

Turn left along the track, the route of the Gritstone Way, to white-painted Bowstones Farm. Just beyond are the Bowstones them-selves. Climb the stile immediately before the farm drive and then the ladder-stile over the wall. Descend the path ahead with the marvellous panorama of the plain stretched out before you. Lyme Hall comes into sight on the right as you drop down to Knightslow Wood. Climb the ladder-stile into the wood and follow the main path through its shade and shelter with glimpses of the house down to the right. Here we heard on one occasion what we claim to be the world's loudest cuckoo – or so it seemed as its calls echoed off the hillside and around the tree trunks.

Leave the wood by ladder-stile and continue down the curving track to the high kissing-gate, negotiation of which may well necessitate removal of your rucksack. At the drive beside the Gritstone Way signpost, you join those who haven't been up to the Bowstones and you bear right towards the wooden café.

Roman Lakes Loop

To descend to Roman Lakes, turn right immediately before the bridge. Drop down the stepped path to the road and continue down the road to the main road. Cross it to descend the drive immediately opposite. Beyond the lower house, the drive becomes a path and the sound of the

River Goyt is heard. Then you are on the riverbank. The path leads to the slender stone arch of a bridge in a delectable wooded valley with an old house just ahead.

You cross the bridge over the Goyt, turn left just before the house (called Roman Lodge but not *that* old!) and make for Roman Lakes along the drive. The river is below you and there is the delicious aniseed smell of massed sweet cicely. The drive takes you past an octagonal lodge and a weir on the river to reach the impressive viaduct of the Manchester to New Mills Central railway line. A breeze and the sound of cascading water had a refreshing effect. Then the main lake appears on the right – with a café that serves ice cream. So turn right if you're roasting. You can even take out a rowing-boat or compete with the geese for the shade under the trees.

But your route continues along the drive, with the lake on the right and railway, canal and Marple on the wooded hill to the left. At the T-junction turn left and, at the next junction of drives, keep straight on along the next drive which then curves sharply left and crosses the river. Immediately after crossing the bridge, go up the narrow path to the right on the left-hand side of the drive. It soon bends back to the left and ascends through the trees.

As you near the treetops, the path is on a wooden cat-walk below the railway and then becomes an attractive path beside the line (a pleasant, shaded, train-spotting refreshment stop on a very hot day). Then the path climbs a bridge over the line, turns left, and ascends to the right to the main road. On the opposite side of the road, a stepped path leads up to the canal, which you cross and then turn right along the towpath with those walking the main route.

Aqueduct Loop and River Goyt Loop

To visit Marple Aqueduct from above, and possibly from below as well, do not continue down the road to the station but, having crossed the canal, turn left along the towpath, beneath great beech trees, down past more locks, where youths were besporting themselves in the doubtless cool but opaque water. With the trees in leaf, this curving flight of locks is a truly beautiful stretch of canal and you have to look hard to see where the railway passes beneath it.

At the foot of the flight, cross the wide bridge to rejoin the towpath on the left bank, under the railway, and out onto the aqueduct. There is an information board illustrating the aqueduct and from the curved parapet near the board you can see something of its elegance. You look 100 feet down through the trees to the river, and, on the other side, the railway viaduct is even higher. A pack of canoeists sped along the canal's narrow ribbon of water as I turned back up the flight to the stile on the left between Locks 1 and 2.

" . . . see the aqueduct and viaduct from below . . . " – Marple

Climb the stile and descend the steps. To walk the River Goyt Loop and see the aqueduct and viaduct from below, turn left along the wide path, down to the foot of the wood, and then left along the edge of the field. At the corner of the field, turn left over a sidestream and along the bank of the river, cross another sidestream, and you are almost under the viaduct with the aqueduct just beyond. Even from below it is not particularly easy to see the aqueduct when the leaves are on the trees. Trains look a long way up. Now make your way back over the two streams, round the edge of the field and up through the wood to the junction of paths near the stile from the canal, to rejoin the Aqueduct Loop.

If you haven't been down to the river, turn right along the level path; if you have, keep straight on along the level path. It bears up to the right and keeps between fence and wall. Follow the path as it keeps between drive and canal and then between drive and railway until you join the drive and cross the railway with it, within sight of the station. Where the drive bears left below the canal and a stepped path descends from the towpath, take the path on the left, bear right above the railway line, left down the road and, finally, left again into the station.

11. RIDGE AND RIVER

Whaley Bridge – Windgather Rocks – Pym Chair – Shining Tor – Errwood Reservoir – Fernilee Reservoir – Taxal – Whaley Bridge.

Distance: between 6 miles and 13 miles.

Starting points:

Whaley Bridge railway station; Outdoor Leisure Map 1, Dark Peak, map reference 011815.

B5470/Reddish Lane junction, Whaley Bridge; Outdoor Leisure Map 1, Dark Peak, map reference 006806.

Pym Chair car park; Outdoor Leisure Map 24, White Peak, map reference 995768.

(You need both maps if you are walking north of Taxal, but otherwise only the White Peak map.)

How to get there:

By car – to Whaley Bridge on the A5004 a mile south of its junction with the A6 between New Mills and Chapel-en-le-Frith. There is a small car park at the station on the right, but it is probably better to continue along the A5004 to its junction with the B5470 and turn right towards Macclesfield for 1/4 mile to Reddish Lane, on the right opposite a telephone box, and park there, to start the walk from there.

- to Pym Chair, continue along the B5470 from Reddish Lane to Kettleshulme, bear left towards the Goyt Valley for another 2 miles and park in the car park on the left just before the T-junction.

By train – to Whaley Bridge on the Manchester to Buxton line.

The title perfectly describes the route of the main walk, for your outward journey is along the super gritstone ridge of Taxal Edge, Windgather Rocks, Cats Tor and Shining Tor. You then descend into the valley of the River Goyt with its utterly different scenery of woods and fields and the two reservoirs of Errwood and Fernilee.

Not only is there great contrast in scenery between the two parts of the walk, but the weather is likely to be different too: I can think of days with strong, chill winds on the ridge ("It's always windy up there," a local told me.) and hot stillness down in the valley. And, the last time I was at Windgather, I was in the cloud and could see no more than 50 yards even after I had wiped my glasses and wrung out my beard.

The full walk is 13 miles long but the two sides of the main route can be easily linked to produce shorter walks. So here is the full repertoire: from Whaley Bridge railway station the full walk is 13 miles, but it's easier to park at Reddish Lane and that reduces it to 11 miles. You could omit the Shining Tor/Errwood Reservoir stretch and that would be 10 miles from Whaley Bridge station or 8 miles from Reddish Lane. Or you could drive all the way to Pym Chair and do a Fernilee Reservoir/ Windgather Rocks circuit of 6 miles or a Shining Tor/Errwood Reservoir circuit (including a visit to the little shrine above Errwood Hall – a delightful diversion) also of 6 miles. Or even put those two circuits together (but not visiting the shrine) and that would be $8^1/_2$ miles.

" . . . *the little shrine above Errwood Hall – a delightful diversion* . . . "

Whichever of those 7 routes you walk, you'll have a share of ridge and river and the contrasts they provide.

The Walk

From the exit on the Buxton-bound platform of Whaley Bridge railway station, turn right and then right again under the bridge. Beyond it, keep straight on up Reservoir Road and the dam of Toddbrook Reservoir will appear before you. Pass the sailing club, heed the "toads crossing" sign, and turn left off the road and over the white-painted bridge across the spillway onto the dam. The reservoir provides water to the Peak Forest Canal. The ridge to the right across the reservoir, Taxal Edge, is your next objective.

A long bridge takes you across a wide overflow, with a warning about the dangers of contamination by blue/green algae when I was last there, so I preferred the pink of willowherb and the yellow of ragwort. At the far end of the dam, you climb the stile in the wall on the right and follow the path to the right beside the hedge. It takes you over a stile in the wall ahead. You keep to the right of the stone farmhouse, take the drive leading to the right, follow it round to the left, and continue along the road ahead, Reddish Lane, to the main road. Here those who have parked in Reddish Lane begin the walk.

Turn right up the main road, past the end of Linglongs Road. Where the main road bears right, bear left up the old road and then follow the drive round to the left. Where the drive then bears right through the gateway to "Taxal Edge", you go through the gate to its left and along the path beneath tall beech trees. The path keeps to the left-hand edge of the field and provides good views to the left to Ladder Hill with the mast on it and back to the left over Whaley Bridge and down the Goyt valley.

At the corner of the field, climb the stile, descend to the road and turn right along it. The road climbs very gently alongside a plantation of conifers, with the Goyt valley to your left, and then the edge of the plantation veers right at a beech tree. Here bear right up the path beside the plantation and with rhododendrons on the left and later on the right as well. As you ascend, you can look back onto Toddbrook Reservoir.

Walk 11

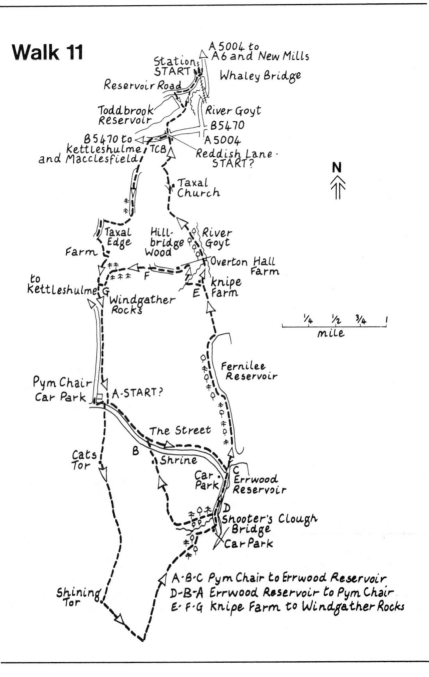

A·B·C Pym Chair to Errwood Reservoir
D·B·A Errwood Reservoir to Pym Chair
E·F·G Knipe Farm to Windgather Rocks

The path curves to the right and makes for the obvious nick in the skyline of Taxal Edge, and you can look back onto the woods along the Goyt. When you reach the ladder-stile in the wall ahead, you're entitled to a couple of minutes' stop to look at the view ahead over Kettleshulme to the Bowstones ridge, beyond which Lyme Park and Greater Manchester are hidden.

To your left are Windgather Rocks, but you've a down and an up before then, so climb the stile and descend the field ahead, bearing slightly right as you do so, aiming for a telegraph pole. You'll find a step-stile and footpath sign beside it. On the road, turn left. The road descends a little and then climbs round a bend. Beyond the bend, climb the stile beside the gate on the left and head up the field to its top corner, to the right of the trees. Over the stile in the wall, keep on to the ladder-stile ahead. Climb that stile, specially designed to deter walkers with little legs and big rucksacks. Go through the wicket-gate, keep to the left of the fence, through the next wicket-gate, and over the next ladder-stile, which causes me the same problems as the previous one.

" . . . *you really are on the rocks, the gritstone of Windgather* . . . "

At the drive, turn left to the farm, through the gate ahead by the old farmhouse, and then turn right through the gateway just beyond the house. Now bear right up the field to the wall and left along the ridge. Through the wall ahead you really are on the rocks, the gritstone of Windgather, you and groups of clinking climbers if my experience is anything to go by. The route of the Fernilee Reservoir/Windgather Rocks circuit from Knipe Farm comes over the ladder-stile on the left.

You are entitled to several minutes' rest here; it always seems to be coffee-time as I look out over the view. You look back along the ridge into the Goyt valley and swing left to a gap through which Greater Manchester can be seen. Then come the Bowstones ridge, the Cheshire plain and the hills beyond, Cats Tor, the head of the Goyt valley and the hills across the river, masted Ladder Hill and Kinder Scout. A party of walkers from Cambridge revealed that they had lost their way and reached Windgather only by not following a public right of way, which just proves you can't trust southerners on northern hills – and that they really need this book!

The sloping slabs form an impressive craggy face below to your right as you proceed, and Goyt Forest fills the valley to your left. Your ridge stretches away ahead. You climb the ladder-stile over the fence ahead and find that, instead of having to walk along the road as the O.S. map suggests, there's a path to the left of the wall, away from the traffic and beside the heather. You can look back to Windgather Rocks, but the best view when I last did this walk was to the left, over the purple heather to the sunlit hills across the Goyt valley.

Immediately after a stone wall goes off to the left and opposite a stile on the right, bear left along the path which follows a line of fence-posts away from the road. I disturbed six grouse enjoying their penultimate day of peace before the "Glorious 12th" – which was to be the 13th, as the 12th was a Sunday!

Go through the remains of a stone wall and up through the heather to a ladder-stile at Pym Chair, a rock which is no longer there. To return to Pym Chair car park, turn right; to descend to Errwood Reservoir without visiting Shining Tor, turn left; but for the full walk keep straight on over the next ladder-stile.

Turn right up the road and left up the rocky steps to the sign to Shining Tor. Look out at the super views over the Cheshire plain, Greater Manchester, and a large chunk of the Peak District. Now, onward along the rising ridge again. As you climb, there are excellent views of crags and cloughs to your right and up to the head of the Goyt valley to your left. And keep looking back to Windgather.

" . . . you can look back to Windgather Rocks . . . "

You climb easily to Cats Tor and, continuing beside the wall, descend with an impressive view of shapely Shutlingsloe beyond the head of the Thursbitch valley to the right of Shining Tor. Then the Post Office tower on Sutton Common appears. A shower swept across and magically misted the ridges. I suspect it was sent to remind me that the climb to Shining Tor is usually a slimy struggle over, through or round sodden peat, when you're not sure whether to keep near the wall or to detour to the left or even on which side of the wall to be at times. Try not to spread the erosion too far to the left and keep enjoying the view back to Cats Tor.

Effort is rewarded soon after you pass the footpath sign for Lamaload Reservoir for, not far beyond, is to be found the trig. point on the summit of Shining Tor. It offers views ahead to Shutlingsloe and Sutton Common with Bosley Cloud and Mow Cop between, out across the

Cheshire plain to the Welsh hills, over Greater Manchester to Winter Hill, and back along the Pennines and over the Peak District.

The Cat and Fiddle pub is on the road ahead, but you're not going there even though you turn left and follow the sign for it. I was amazed that, as I descended by the wall on my last visit, the peat was so dusty-dry that I had no need to use the bridges and boardwalks; you may not be so lucky. In the interests of preventing erosion, the path has been surfaced with chippings for part of the descent and the climb to the next ridge.

It leads you to a stile, beyond which you turn left along the path on the new ridge, where, on a recent visit, I had a most interesting chat with the gamekeeper for Lord Derby, who has the shooting rights on these moors. I think the view as you gently descend is gorgeous, with the blue waters of Errwood Reservoir, the golden-green of the moorland grass, the dark green of the plantations, and the rise and fall of the hills. To the left, the ridge along which I'd just walked was purpled with ling.

The track takes you between two stone gateposts and I rather favour this bit of hillside for a lunch spot, although it may be more sheltered lower down. Lunch over, continue to descend by the wall. When you reach the ladder-stile on the left, do not climb it but bear right along the path down the hillside, still aiming for Errwood Reservoir. You descend to climb a ladder-stile and continue downhill beyond it, with Foxlow Edge to your left and Windgather farther to the left.

Where the path forks, bear left to keep near the edge of the left-hand wood, through a patch of bracken. The path keeps to the right of a fine larch with two trunks. It then turns left across a wall, and then descends to the right, through a gateway with massive stone gateposts, and down to a car park – with benches and tables if you want a civilised lunch-spot, probably in the company of real human beings, not walkers, so you'll need to mind your manners. There's a useful information board at the car park too.

Turn left along the road above the reservoir and across Shooter's Clough bridge. Those returning to Pym Chair via the shrine will climb the steps beyond the bridge. All others continue along the road to the next car park, to be joined there by those who have walked down beside the road from Pym Chair.

Take the road to the right towards the dam of Errwood Reservoir but, before you reach the dam, take the gently-rising track on the left by the footpath sign. Leave it just beyond the second tree, where another footpath sign points to the right. Obey it and, where the path forks after a few yards, keep to the left along the hillside and through the wall. Then descend through the wood to the bank of Fernilee Reservoir, with the outflow from Errwood noisy to your right.

Over the ladder-stile or through the gate, continue along the track above the reservoir. Bleached tree-trunks lie like ancient bones at the water's edge. Keep along the track, which narrows in places but you cannot mistake it. Look for the wrap-around root of an oak tree on the right just after crossing one of the sidestreams.

If in doubt, keep to the path nearest the water's edge. The dam will appear, seeming not far ahead. Eventually your path will swing left uphill and you will arrive at a track, along which you turn right. At last you climb a stile and leave the wood to turn right along the road towards the dam of Fernilee Reservoir. Do not cross that dam either, though you are welcome to venture onto it far enough to look back to the head of the reservoir.

Your route lies along the farm drive on the left before the dam, with a view ahead down a far less wild and rugged Goyt valley. You pass a magnificent oak with its branches down to the ground and go through a kissing-gate beside a gate across the drive. Where the drive bears left, you continue along it only if bound for Windgather and Pym Chair. To return to Whaley Bridge, you take the footpath straight on to the wicket-gate in the wall on the right. Through the gate, turn left along by the wall and then bear right along the right-hand side of the old hedge beyond Knipe Farm. A stile then leads you into a sunken path which can be very wet. The path continues beyond a gate and curves attractively round to the right and back to the left to deliver you at a footbridge over the stream from Mill Clough near its confluence with the River Goyt. It's very pretty.

Continue along the riverbank, over the stile ahead, and then over the one on the left; do not go over the bridge across the river. The sign says you are in Hillbridge Wood Nature Reserve, so sit on the bench and appreciate it.

Physically and spiritually refreshed, continue along the path through the meadows and up into the wood. This beautiful wood is complete with its own stream – and rabbits. The path winds its way to the top of the wood and leaves it by a stile, from where you can see the nick in Taxal Edge through which you went this morning.

Follow the path ahead between the stone gateposts and then bearing left to a sign ahead in the corner of the field. You meet a drive and keep on down it. Follow the fenced drive past a stone farm and Taxal's tucked-away church with yews in the churchyard and wrought-iron gates bearing rams' heads and the scallop-shell symbol of St. James. Beyond the church, do not bear left along the road, but keep straight on along the gravel drive to the right of the houses and then along the path beyond, through the trees.

Climb the rustic stile and keep on up the path and across the drive. The path continues on the far side, climbs a stile, and bears left across a field, then back to the right, and finally left along the edge of the field, with Whaley Bridge now prominent. The path takes you up to the road by the telephone box, near which your car may be parked.

For Whaley Bridge station, cross the road and retrace your outward route along Reddish Lane, right to the farm, left of the house, over the stile ahead and along the path to the beginning of the dam. Go mad at the end of the walk and do something outrageous! So, instead of turning left over the dam to follow your outward route, be different and climb the wooden stile ahead and turn left along the path below the dam. The path takes you gently down and round to the right and onto a tarmac path. Turn left at the first tarmac junction, straight on at the second, across the metal footbridge over Todd Brook, past the playground on your left with the Goyt on your right, and up the path to Reservoir Road.

Continue along the road to the railway bridge and turn left to the station. If you want the Manchester platform, you don't even need to cross under the line as there's an entrance from Whaley Lane – and a good job too as, when I last did this walk, I had only half a minute to spare before the train arrived.

Pym Chair to Errwood Reservoir

From the car park, walk on to the T-junction and turn left towards the Goyt valley. Keep along the left side of the road. For Shining Tor, cross the road to the footpath sign on the right but, for Errwood, continue beside the road known as The Street, between fence and wall and along the off-the-road path. Stricken larches provide sheep-shelter and there was a peacock butterfly parading as monarch of the thistles. As you descend towards the Goyt, there are trees on both sides of the road.

Continue on the left of the road until you reach the car park by the road junction. Turn left along the road towards the dam, now on the route of the main walk.

Errwood Reservoir to Pym Chair

After crossing Shooter's Clough Bridge, climb the flight of steps on the left and follow the path uphill through rhododendrons and between handsome pines and larches, a legacy of Errwood Hall. The path passes a red waymark and arrives at a vertical log notice-board. Descend to the left here to the next red waymark and keep along the broad path until you reach the bridge over the stream. Just before it, a yellow waymark with a "2" on it points to the right, and that's the way you go.

The path creeps under a sweet chestnut and then keeps on along the valley side. Stick to path 2 as it gradually climbs and then levels off. Trees rise up from the stream and there is a ruined building on the right. Then take the left fork in the path down to the little shrine, erected by the Grimshawes of Errwood Hall in memory of a Spanish governess. Enter in peace by the low door, give thanks for a safe journey and its continuation as a mediaeval traveller would have done, and then, having shut the door as you leave, climb the steps behind the little building and turn left along the path up to the road. Cross to the path on the far side and turn left back to Pym Chair car park.

Knipe Farm to Windgather Rocks

Continue along the drive past Knipe Farm and down the grassy track beyond, into Mill Clough. Go through the kissing-gate beside the big gate, cross the stream, and follow the track to the right. This pretty, walled track leads up to Madscar Farm (where the farmer rushed out to display a notice telling us that his plums were only 20p a pound – and very good they were). At the farm, go through the left-hand gate and up another walled track. Swing left with it at the hair-pin bend, with views down into the Goyt valley.

It's an easy climb up to Overton Hall Farm, with a bench on the way. Beyond the farm, continue up the drive beside the right-hand wall. You cross a cattle-grid and the drive turns right, but you keep on up the footpath opposite. The path maintains a straight course up the hillside, nears the wood on the left, and takes you over the ridge to reach a stone wall across the path.

Do not go over the stile in the wall but bear left to the ladder-stile. Climb it and follow the path along the edge of the wood to the waymark. There turn left beside the fence and into the wood. Keep near that left-hand fence, crossing a little stream by a sleeper-bridge, and climbing to a bench and a ladder-stile. Sit on the bench if you wish, but there's not much more climbing to do. Over the ladder-stile on the left, keep between wood and wall. When the wall turns right uphill, you and the path follow it over the next ladder-stile and up onto the edge of Windgather Rocks, where you turn left along the route of the main walk.

12. LIMESTONE AND LINES

Wyedale – Cheedale – Miller's Dale – Monk's Dale – Tideswell – Miller's Dale – Blackwell – Wyedale.

Distance: between $5^1/_2$ miles and 13 miles.

Starting points:

Wyedale car park, Topley Pike; Outdoor Leisure Map 24, White Peak, map reference 104725.

Miller's Dale station; Outdoor Leisure Map 24, White Peak, map reference 138733.

How to get there:

By car – to Wyedale car park on the left-hand side of the A6 opposite Topley Pike Quarry, about 3 miles east of Buxton between Buxton and Bakewell.

- for Miller's Dale station car park, turn left onto the B6049 (for Tideswell) off the A6 between Buxton and Bakewell and immediately after crossing the river in Miller's Dale turn left up to Miller's Dale station car park.

By bus – from Manchester to Topley Pike Quarry, between Buxton and Taddington, but note that the bus-service is a 2-hourly one.

This is a dramatic walk in a distinctive landscape – and a distinctive walk in a dramatic landscape! It explores the contrasts in the heart of the White Peak's limestone by threading its way through the chasm of Cheedale and Miller's Dale beside and above the River Wye, and sometimes almost in it, turns up fascinating Monk's Dale with its National Nature Reserve and then follows lines of stiles across lines of drystone, limestone walls to and from the lovely little town of Tideswell with its superb church, "The Cathedral of the Peak", and back from Miller's Dale to Wyedale again over the limestone plateau with stupendous views down into Cheedale.

Part of the excitement is following stretches of the former Midland Railway line from St. Pancras to Manchester, through tunnels and over viaducts. I remember thrilling journeys by steam train over those viaducts and in and out of the tunnels in a wreath of smoke ("Change at Miller's Dale for Buxton") and it may be possible again if Peak Rail have their way, but at the moment walking is the best possible substitute.

And there is more excitement when the path through Cheedale takes to stepping-stones on the riverbed because there is no room for a path on the riverbank – so don't try the walk when the river is high. It *is* a rough path through Cheedale and also through Monk's Dale, but you should cope if you take things slowly.

The full walk is 13 miles in length. If you're using the bus, you need to do either the full walk or the $5^1/_2$-mile Cheedale circuit from Wyedale but, if you've travelled by car, you could park at Miller's Dale and do either a $5^1/_2$-mile Cheedale circuit or a $6^1/_2$-mile Tideswell circuit if you didn't want to do the full walk. And, if you're using the bus, note that they are only every 2 hours. I think this is such a thrilling walk that I've made an exception to my general rule for this book that there should be at least an hourly bus or train to the start.

So go – and be thrilled.

The Walk

Walk through the Wyedale car park and along the drive beyond. It follows the River Wye as it curves along its dale, below trees and through a jungle of butterbur leaves. When I was last here, there were mallard and coot on the water and a red-berried column of wild arum beside it. The railway leaps from one side of the valley to the other, still in use here as a link between Buxton and the limestone quarries in Great Rocks Dale.

Just before the third viaduct, climb the stepped path on the right. If you haven't been counting, don't worry; just look for that stepped path on the right before *a* viaduct, with a Monsal Trail sign beside it, and climb the path to the old railway line. Turn right along the line, which has a noisy, ballast surface. To your left is Great Rocks Dale and ahead is a cutting. (You may be joined here by those walking the Cheedale circuit from Miller's Dale station.)

Walk 12

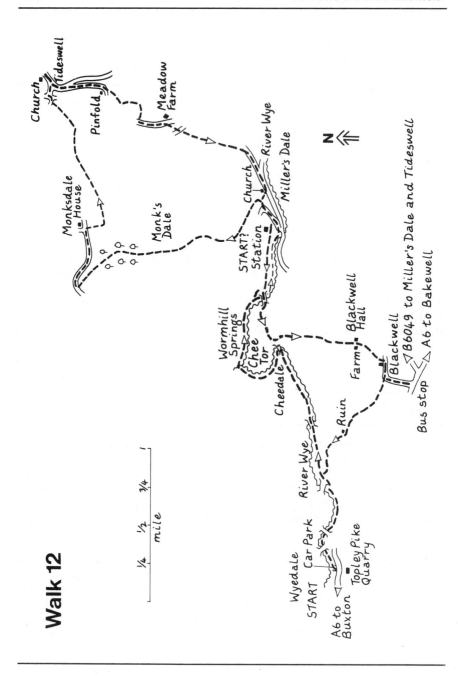

The track-side was blue and yellow with scabious and hawkweed as cliffs towered above me on the right and across the river to the left. The track becomes more grassy and your footsteps therefore quieter. You cross a viaduct over the river so that you are now on the north side of the valley and can look down on the river before going through Rusher Cutting Tunnel in a spur of cliff. This short tunnel makes very obvious the scale of the civil engineering works involved in the construction of the line. On a different scale, but no less wonderful, the flowers of the cranesbill were in bloom but their leaves were turning red as summer drew to a close.

As I approached the next tunnel, Chee Tor No. 2, cows silhouetted on the cliff-edge up ahead looked in imminent danger of death. Later, you may be up there with the cows. Beyond that tunnel, you cross the river again and then your way along the track is blocked as you cannot proceed through the next tunnel, a lengthy one. So take the signed path to the right. It leads down steps to a T-junction of paths, where you turn right to continue downstream again. You descend to river-level, pass under the viaduct you have just crossed, and then cross the river by footbridge.

Now comes the interesting bit where the valley is so narrow that the path is along a line of stepping-stones on the bed of the river at the foot of a cliff. Back on dry land, you walk under a high cliff which leans out in overhangs above you. Climbers were about to ascend and I should like to have stopped to see if they took their dog with them or left it behind to guard their packs. Then came a couple of climbers with a baby, but the wife assured me the baby was just to help with the belay!

The path is narrow and rough below the cliff and then it descends to the river again and is smooth but muddy. On the opposite bank, climbers were distributed across the face of Chee Tor. It is exciting here hemmed in by 300-foot high ramparts of rock. By means of a rocky staircase the path climbs up from the river. Soon a footbridge leads over the stream from Flag Dale. The path goes over a stone stile, bears right to another bridge, passes the bubbling waters of Wormhill Springs, a mass of yellow mimulus when I was last here, and keeps down by the river.

Another stone stairway leads you upwards and then you descend gradually to a much more open stretch of the valley, pretty rather than dramatic. Here beds of knapweed and meadowsweet were in flower and in the river were forget-me-nots and water crowfoot. Pass the metal footbridge over the river and continue along the riverside path, where there were wonderfully-green reflections in the still water.

Another viaduct strides across the river – and you may have to dodge abseilers dropping off it. To return to Wyedale on the Cheedale circuit, climb the steeply-stepped path on the left before the viaduct and turn right across it with those coming from Miller's Dale station. Otherwise continue along the riverbank to emerge on a minor road in Miller's Dale near its junction with the B6049.

Turn left up the minor road, under the railway bridges, to café, car park and conveniences. Here you will end your walk if you started from here to do only the Cheedale circuit; if starting the Tideswell circuit from here, turn left up the road as you leave the car park; and, if doing the full walk from Wyedale, continue up the road.

At the sharp bend before white-painted Glebe Farm, turn right over the stile beside the footpath sign, along by the wall and through the gate into Monk's Dale National Nature Reserve. Bear slightly left from the gate and you will see the path descending to the left and down into the dale, with views away ahead of you. The path swings right, steeply downhill, and then left to join a much better path on the valley floor. Turn left along it away from Miller's Dale.

The path crosses a footbridge (though there was no stream when I last did this walk) and turns left to keep on up the dale, where the several paths all seem to go to the same place. Try rubbing the leaves of the water mint for a delicious smell.

One path keeps down in the bottom of the valley (on the right of the wall) and the other climbs the shoulder of limestone on the right. It doesn't matter which you take as far as the wall-corner where they rejoin. This wonderfully sinuous dale was utterly peaceful apart from an occasional bird calling out a warning at my approach.

You descend rocky steps into ashwood, climb a stile in a stone wall and continue along the path deep down on the wooded floor of the dale. It's a fascinating stretch of path but it is rough, slippery, bouldery and ankle-twisting, so great care is needed. You leave the reserve at the next stile but continue up the dale, at last open and unthreatening again, to the road.

Turn right along the road out of the valley. As you climb, there is a very fine view to the right down into Monk's Dale. At the road junction by

Monksdale House, turn right along the walled track on the route of the Limestone Way. By the Peak and Northern Footpaths Society signpost on the left, climb the stile; it's in the fourth field on the left after leaving the road.

Bear slightly right to find the stile ahead in the corner of the field. Pass a concrete dewpond and make for the gate and footpath sign at the top of the field. From the stile there is a wonderful view over the limestone uplands with their pattern of stone walls. As I stood here on a recent visit, the sound of the bells came over the fields from the still-hidden church in Tideswell and I felt like a mediaeval traveller being guided to safety.

Cross the grassy lane, bear left to the next stile and then two more, and now follow the line of stiles ahead until you reach the walled track. Turn left along it and the tower of the church will appear ahead. You arrive at the attractive houses and gardens of Tideswell, with glimpses over grey rooftops to the tower of the church. Turn right at the first road and left

" . . . glimpses over grey rooftops to the tower of the church . . . " – Tideswell

at the second, right at the third junction (by the Congregational school) – the church tower is nearer now – and finally left along the main road to the church. There are cafés and other facilities in the delightful buildings around the church.

Retrace your steps along the main street as far as the war memorial and there bear right along the road parallel to the main street and in front of the Methodist church. Keep on along this back road until, just past the sign for the pinfold on the right, you reach a T-junction, and the back road continues as the drive into a farm. Do not go into the farm but turn right up the road, Richard Lane, left into the children's playground (well, alright then, just a few minutes' playtime) and out through the stile in its top corner.

Bear right to the next stile, in the same direction to the third, more to the right for the fourth, and then straight on beside the left-hand wall until you have passed through a small, rough field, probably with a muck-heap in it. There turn right along the walled track to the road and turn left down it.

Opposite the gate to Meadow Farm down in the dip, climb the stile on the right and ascend by the wall. The path pursues a straight course over a succession of stiles, crossing a road and a walled track. Tideswell Dale is to the left and then Miller's Dale appears impressively ahead. Don't miss the stile to the right of the gateway to the right of the group of trees and then the stile beyond that. From there the slightly sunken path takes you down to a gateway. Then keep just to the right of the dewpond to a stile onto the road, and turn right downhill into Miller's Dale.

At the main road, turn right, note the mill wheel on the left, and then, immediately beyond the church, turn right up the path signed for Monk's Dale. It winds up steps to a gate and there you turn left so as not to go into Monk's Dale but up to the road at Glebe Farm. Turn left down the road and then right, opposite the café, to Miller's Dale station.

To continue the walk back to Wyedale, or to start the Cheedale circuit from here, go onto the old railway line and turn right past the platforms. The track is a bit too civilised here, but you can add some excitement by bearing right up the path to the top of the lime kilns. Keep on along the track at the foot of the kilns and onto the viaduct over the Wye, where your route is joined by those doing the Cheedale circuit from Wyedale – and you can all watch the abseilers disappearing over the parapet.

Just across the viaduct, turn right over the stile by the gate and follow the path to the next gate and stile. About 50 yards beyond them, just past the scanty remains of a building on the left, look for a path which bears left into the hawthorn bushes and joins a more obvious path. Follow that path up to the right. Keep on bearing right gently uphill rather than taking the path which turns steeply up to the left level with the spoilheap on the left.

When you reach bare limestone, the path, less clear now, bears left, with a good view back into the dale and down to Miller's Dale station. Follow the path up over the hill – it's clear enough – until you arrive at a wall at a most dramatic spot overlooking Cheedale. The river's course has curved round below Chee Tor. You follow the wall to the left above it until you can stand where those silhouetted cows were, directly above the tunnel entrance and looking up the dale along the line with its two short tunnels where you were near the start of the walk. Last time I stood here I watched a climber on the cliff above the stepping-stones and a kestrel quartering the ground below me.

" . . . a most dramatic spot overlooking Cheedale . . . "

Keep round the wall of this field to the left until you reach a gap with a waymark and there turn right. Follow the left-hand wall to the stile and, over that, keep up by the right-hand wall. At the top of the field, turn right and then left along the walled track up to Blackwell Hall Farm.

Beyond the last farm building on the right, a large concrete shed, the drive bears left, but you bear right along a path among stones and through the line of trees. The path leads to a hole in the wall and you follow the wall ahead to a wooden stile. From there, bear right to the stile in the wall, climb it, bear left to the next stile and, over that, bear left into the narrow finger of field which leads beside the farm to the road.

Now turn right along the road, past the farm with the unexpected telephone box. Where the road turns left, stop and think, if you are wanting to catch the bus back to Buxton and beyond. By the route of the walk, it's more than a mile back to Wyedale; can you get there in time for the next bus to avoid a 2-hour wait? If not, it's less than $^1/_4$ mile along the road to the left to the bus route on the A6.

If you've got time, or you're not dependent on the bus, don't turn left along the road, but keep straight on over the stile beside the right-hand gate and take the walled track ahead. At the end of the track, follow the path ahead, to the left of the ruin, over the stile and across to the right to the stile on the left just before the field corner. Climb it and make for the corner ahead where the next stile takes you outside the fields. Here, in a sea of scabious, you can make your way to the edge of the cliff for vertiginous views, but try to avoid looking over at man's mess in Great Rocks Dale.

The right of way turns left along the wall, descends ahead from the wall-corner, and turns right along the left-hand side of the spur between the side-valley on the left and the main valley on the right. Don't be tempted to do what I did the first time I used this path and was in a hurry to get back to the bus stop; I carried on right to the end of the spur and finished up with a rock-scramble that I found too worrying to be enjoyable. Make sure you look out for – and use – the narrow, zigzag path which drops down to the left into the side-valley. It's just after a low hawthorn bush on the left and opposite the path which comes down the far side of the side-valley, from the lay-by on the A6.

At the foot of that path, turn right down the broad path and go over the stile to the left of the bridge over the old railway. Descend to the line and turn right if you're making for Miller's Dale but left to return to

Wyedale. Then it's left down the steps to the riverside track and left along that back to the car park at Wyedale, with the bus stop along to the right beyond the quarry entrance. I hope you've not too long to wait for a bus and that it's not full when it arrives.

13. PUFF AND PERFECTION

Hope – Aston – Win Hill – Townhead – Lose Hill – Back Tor – Hope.

Distance: between 6 miles and $10^1/_2$ miles.

Starting point: Hope railway station; Outdoor Leisure Map 1, Dark Peak, map reference 182833.

How to get there:

By car – to Hope on the A625 between Chapel-en-le-Frith and Hathersage. Beyond Hope church, turn up the second road on the left to Hope railway station.

By train – to Hope on the Manchester to Sheffield line.

Perfect, pointed peaks are an attraction to climbers and walkers. Unfortunately the Matterhorn is more than 25 miles from the centre of Manchester, but the Peak District does include some quite sharply-pointed hills offering a sense of achievement and an all-round view from the summit. This walk visits two of them – Win Hill and Lose Hill on opposite sides of the valley of the River Noe between Hope and Edale. Both peaks can seem a long way up from the valley and you'll need two lots of puff for the complete walk of $10^1/_2$ miles. You can tackle them separately with a 6-mile walk to the top of Win Hill and a $7^1/_2$-mile walk to Lose Hill.

I hope you will be as lucky with the weather as I was when I last did this walk. A warm spring day offered a cooling breeze on top, excellent visibility and marvellous colouring of sky, water, valleys and hills. That was perfection. But it was jolly hot climbing and that used a lot of puff!

The Walk

From the car park at Hope station, cross the footbridge and turn right along the path on the far side of the line. Or, from the Sheffield-bound platform, go up the steps to the first landing on the bridge, down to the left and along the footpath. The summit of Win Hill is visible above you.

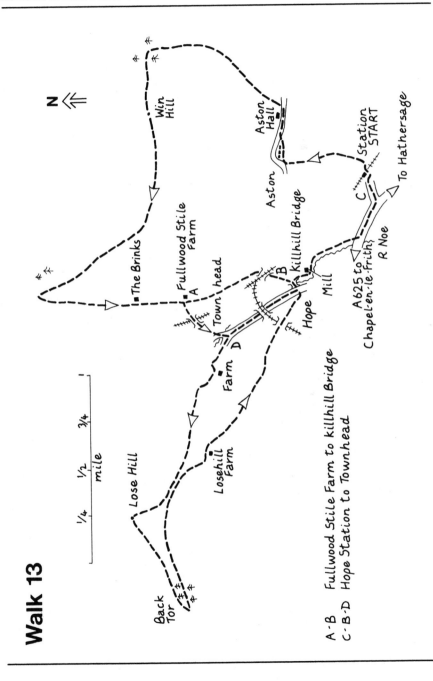

Walk 13

A - B   *Fullwood Stile Farm to killhill Bridge*
C - B - D   *Hope Station to Townhead*

Through the kissing-gate, follow the path by the right-hand hedge. The summit of Lose Hill can be seen through the trees to the left, and to its left Back Tor and Mam Tor come into view. Follow the path beside the stream with the summit rocks of Win Hill up ahead. There's even a signpost to Win Hill. The Great Ridge from Lose Hill to Rushup Edge does look impressive to the left, and Bradwell Edge and Shatton Moor are behind you. The less said about the cement works the better!

When you reach the road among the scattering of houses that is Aston, turn right along it for a few paces and then turn right along the drive. Do not turn left up to the house but go through the gate ahead into the field (where there were very young lambs on my last visit), through the next gateway, and along by the left-hand wall to the stile, beyond which you drop down steps to the road.

Keep on along the road, uphill, with doves in the air and on the gateposts. Aston Hall is handsome on the left. Beyond it the road descends and you turn up the track on the left beside the stone troughs. Over the stile, the path begins to climb by the right-hand hedge and the slope of Win Hill looks daunting. Two tiny lambs were engaging in head-butting practice – very gently.

The long, thin pasture narrows to a stile, from where you look right, down the Derwent valley towards Grindleford and the Edges. Now bear slightly right to the ladder-stile in the wall at the top of the field and, beyond that, take the clear path which bears right up the hillside. The super view down the Derwent valley gives you an excuse to keep stopping – to let other people catch up, of course. The Derwent winds its meanders below you. Keep on along the main path, with Ladybower Reservoir now in view.

Win Hill's summit appears to the left but you don't turn up to it yet. You keep on the pleasant, level path through the heather, bear right through the wall, and on along the track ahead with the stone wall on your left.

When you reach the wood, turn up the path on the left (just after a stile on the right) and plod steadily uphill through beeches and larches and out into the heather again. The summit rocks appear, you struggle over a ladder-stile, and then you make the final assault. On that rocky top, the view makes you realise it's all worthwhile. Ahead of you is the Great Ridge of Lose Hill, Back Tor and Mam Tor. You can look round to Castleton with Peveril Castle on its crag to the left of the village, Shatton

Moor and the Derwent valley, the Edges, the two branches of Ladybower Reservoir, and Kinder Scout.

" . . .on that rocky top . . . " – Win Hill

If the weather's good, this place is a must for your coffee-break, for you can drink in the view as well. Now descend from the rocks and continue towards Lose Hill. Hope village, with its spired church, and that unmentionable cement works are down to your left.

Keep to that main path along the ridge, past the signpost, and don't be tempted by the path to the left signposted to Lose Hill. The ridge is too good to leave yet, as the view past Castleton reveals the great gash of the Winnats Pass, and you can keep looking back to the summit rocks.

You reach walls, keep on alongside the one ahead until it ends and then stay on the obvious track which bears slightly right. The track winds on along the ridge, displaying your path up Lose Hill. Edale is revealed to the right of Lose Hill and Rushup Edge is behind Mam Tor. This gently-descending track is a particularly marvellous stretch of walking when the heather is in bloom.

You pass through a stone wall, with serried ranks of conifers to your right, and drop down for less than 100 yards to where a path crosses the track. Turn left along that path, heading straight for the summit of Lose Hill. The path soon swings left and it's good for train-spotting, though you need jolly good eyesight to see the numbers.

The path takes you easily down and round the hillside to join the Hope Cross track at a gate. Go through the gate and follow the lane, perhaps with violets in flower on the banks, past The Brinks, with its superb view across to Lose Hill. The lane bears right at the entrance to Fullwood Stile Farm. To return to Hope, go into the farm, but to continue the walk to Lose Hill bear right with the lane, cross the railway line, join the road and go straight ahead over Townhead Bridge across the River Noe.

Then turn back up the first road on the right, with those who have come straight from Hope station. When the road forks, you climb left, with your path down the side of Win Hill clear across the valley. The drive turns left to Townhead Farm, but you go over the stile on the right and up the fenced and tree-lined path. As you approach the next stile, the summit of Lose Hill is before you, and quite a lot higher.

The path keeps by the wall and you grit your teeth and keep going. Ascent seemed easier for the hang-glider over on Win Hill. Soon you can look back down the Derwent valley to the Edges, and by the time you reach the next stile Win Hill's summit rocks are in view behind you.

The climb up the well-worn path eases off now and the summit of Lose Hill looks quite close, as do the trees on Back Tor. Across the Hope valley the castle sits above Castleton. Beyond the final stile, there's just that last pull up to the top of Lose Hill.

The slope eases off before too long and the far side of the summit reveals the best view, the one you've not had on the ascent – looking over the whole of the long valley of Edale, across to the great amphitheatre of Grindsbrook Clough, and along to Edale Head and the watershed between the North Sea and the Irish Sea. You can look back to Win Hill, then across the full length of the Hope valley and down the Derwent.

Then continue along the ridge towards Mam Tor and Rushup Edge. The ridge descends to a stile and then the path is between fence and wall. The path continues to descend and then rises gently to the top of Back

Tor; you'll hardly notice the ascent after conquering Lose Hill. Grindsbrook and Crowden Cloughs are impressive to the north of Edale.

Follow the rough path steeply down until you are level with the end of the wood. Then descend by the fence on the left, over the stile on the right, and back to the left over the next stile. Your route is now along the level path through Brocket Booth Plantation, heading for Win Hill.

Over the stile at the end of the wood, keep parallel to the wall on the left as you ascend a little towards Lose Hill (don't worry, you're not going to the top again!) and then, when the wall veers left, follow the path ahead climbing hardly at all. Stiles in the cross-walls confirm you're on the right route and you can watch people on the skyline struggling to the top of Lose Hill. That's very satisfying.

You'll find this path under the ridge much less populous than the one on top – and the larks sound more personal. Note on the ground and on the $2^1/_2$ inch map the strange rounded stone wall on your right.

Beyond that rounded area, you have a straight wall on your left. At the end of that wall, you climb a stile, look back to the impressive view of Back Tor and the Winnats Pass, and then make for the large cairn with Win Hill behind it. At the standing stone before that cairn, turn right along the near side of the remains of the stone wall. Your path upward was on the other side of the wall.

You follow the path when it bears right, away from the wall, to the upper end of a group of trees and straight for that cement works I'm not mentioning. It's better to look at Shatton Moor on the port bow and Castleton and Mam Tor to starboard. The terraced path curves round to the left to keep above the buildings of Losehill Farm and arrives at a stile and signpost.

Over that stile, climb the ladder-stile on the right (it's a long way down), then keep by the right-hand wall. At the end of the wall, bear left to the stile to the right of the stone barn. Cross the stile, keep by the left-hand wall and fence and, if you're tiring, note that Hope is increasing.

Shortly after the end of the wall, climb the stile on the left, walk the plank in the stream, and bear right down the field to the stile beside the tallest tree. There is a good view ahead to Bradwell Edge. The path descends beside the ditch for a couple of fields, then keeps to the left of a wooded gully. It then goes through a kissing-gate and along the right-hand side of the field to a stile. This leads to a hedge-lined lane along which you turn left, with Win Hill now looking high above you.

The path leaves the lane where it's overgrown and continues beside it. Beyond the next stile, the path takes you between buildings and becomes a drive. Where that turns left, go through the stile ahead and over the footbridge across the cement works' railway line. Cross the field ahead, and the summit rocks of Win Hill appear up on the left – tempting you to go round again?

You cross a series of narrow fields with Lose Hill now impressive behind you. Go through a wicket-gate and turn left through a similar one to keep to the right of a black corrugated-iron barn. Climb the step-stile in the bottom right-hand corner of the field and go through the squeezer-stile to emerge on the road.

Cross it and turn left down the road on the far side to reach Killhill Bridge over the River Noe. Now turn right along the track on the far bank, joined by those who've come from Fullwood Stile Farm. The track runs between river and mill-leat and keeps on the river-side of the old mill, which still has its water-wheel. Go left round the far side of the mill and, opposite the garages, there is a stile on the right leading to the continuation of the path.

Keep along by the right-hand hedge, first above the leat and then above the river. Climb the steps up onto the bridge, and turn left along the main road, past the lane to Aston. Then turn left up Station Road to – you guessed? – Hope station, with its views of Win Hill and Lose Hill. The best view of Lose Hill and the Great Ridge is from the centre of the bridge, made, according to the elegant scroll, about a mile from my childhood home. As I sat on the station waiting for my train, a curlew called; that's the sort of station I like.

Fullwood Stile Farm to Killhill Bridge

To return to Hope, go into Fullwood Stile Farm and follow the track to the right of the stone buildings, climb the stile on the right, and turn along by the left-hand hedge. The waiting cement wagons are not very beautiful but Lose Hill is. Beyond the trio of trees, keep on by the left-hand fence and wall and along the drive.

" . . .the best view of Lose Hill and the Great Ridge is from the centre of the bridge . . . " –
Hope station

Stay on the drive as it swings right under the railway line and left beyond it, and down to the River Noe. Turn left along the track on the near bank to join those who have been up Lose Hill.

Hope Station to Townhead

From the Sheffield-bound platform of Hope station, cross the bridge and turn right along the road and down to the main road. Again turn right, pass the end of the road to Aston, and then go through the gap in the right-hand parapet of the bridge over the River Noe. Steps lead down into the field and you keep by its left-hand edge, above the river and then the mill-leat, to arrive at the old mill.

Follow the drive round to its left and then upstream between river and leat to the road. Turn left over Killhill Bridge and then through the stile on the right and up the footpath. Now turn right along the road, passing the weir that provided the head of water for the mill. On your left is the

144   *Rambles around Manchester*

Cheshire Cheese Inn, but you're not entitled to turn aside and enter as you've not been up Win Hill. And, by my evil design, those who *have* been up Win Hill don't pass the inn!

Walk under the railway line to the cement works and look out for Townhead House on the right, for your route is up the road which bears left just beyond, and that's where you join those doing the full walk.

14. FALL AND FOUNTAIN

Hayfield – Snake Path – Kinder Downfall – Wool Packs – Edale Cross – Hayfield.

Distance: 10 miles or 12 miles.

Starting point:

Hayfield bus station; Outdoor Leisure Map 1, Dark Peak, map reference 037869.

How to get there:

By car – to Hayfield at the junction of the A624 and the A6015 between Glossop and Chapel-en-le-Frith. From the A624 turn onto the A6015 and then turn down Station Road, the first road on the right, to the bus station and car park (or, if coming on the A6015 from New Mills, Station Road is the last on the left before the junction with the A624).

By train and bus – either by train from Manchester to Stockport and then by bus from Stockport bus station to Hayfield bus station or by train from Manchester to New Mills Newtown on the Manchester to Buxton line and then by bus from the forecourt of the railway station to Hayfield bus station.

This walk, which will be well-known to afficionados of the Peak District, includes no easy alternative, for its goal is high on the exposed edge of the Kinder Scout plateau. And that goal is . . . ? The waterfall at Kinder Downfall where the River Kinder throws itself over the great, gritstone escarpment in the hope of joining the River Sett and then the Goyt and finally the Mersey to reach the Irish Sea. But it doesn't always succeed, for a strong wind will turn fall into fountain and hurl it back up the cliff and high into the air like smoke from a burgeoning bonfire. It's a thrilling sight which amply justifies the 10 miles of the main walk, with the pull up William Clough.

If one goal isn't enough, you could undertake a diversion of another 2 miles to the strange rocks of the Wool Packs, which offer drama, humour, mystery . . . . All human life is there, or is it death that stalks the hillside? What will your reaction be, I wonder?

There is no easy alternative and conditions on Kinder can be very harsh, so do take appropriate precautions: be properly clad and shod, and choose your day for a great experience.

The Walk

From the car park and bus station – and information centre – use the crossing or subway to reach the church on the far side of the A624. Beyond the church turn left over the bridge across the River Sett and then turn right up Bank Street behind the bank. There are interesting shops, eating-places and old houses to enjoy on your journey through the village, and look out for the unexpected Old Grammar School on the right.

Continue along the "main" road beyond it and then, after a couple of hundred yards, climb the flight of steps after house number 121 on the left. There is a splendid Peak and Northern Footpaths Society sign. The track bears up to the left and then swings right. It continues unmistakably upward between fences and you can look back onto the rooftops of Hayfield.

The path takes you up past a group of trees, with the Sett valley leading to New Mills to the left. Through the kissing-gate at the corner of the field with the trees, keep by the left-hand wall and then follow the path as it bears up to the right above the wooded valley containing the road to Glossop. You can now look left to The Cage in Lyme Park and across the Mersey plain.

Through the next kissing-gate, keep by the wall again as the path rounds the hillside and continue as it curves right, up a valley to another kissing-gate. Beyond it you are told that you are within the boundary of open country, on National Trust land, and following the Snake Path. Ahead the skyline will soon be your route. When I last stood here, the sun broke through the clouds and spotlit Kinder Downfall dramatically. The cries of curlew confirmed that it was "open country".

The path takes you easily up towards the white shooting hut. You don't go over the long footbridge to the left but keep to the right of the hut with views back, on each side of Lantern Pike, to the plain and Greater Manchester. By the plethora of signs, keep right, with a super view up

Walk 14

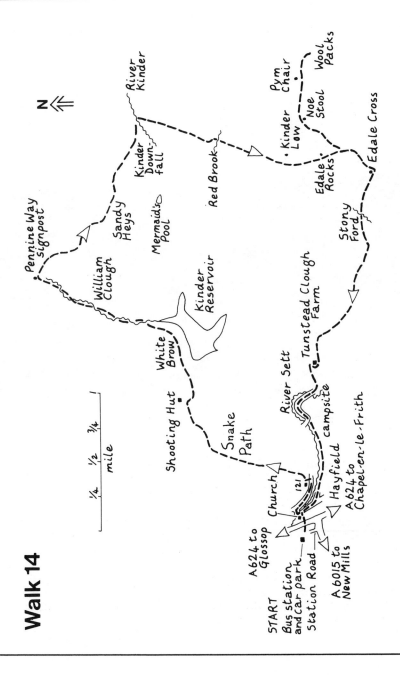

the Sett valley to South Head on the right, but do not take the bridleway leading downhill to the right.

" . . . a super view up the Sett valley to South Head . . . "

Your route now curves round to the left along White Brow, above Kinder Reservoir in its bowl of hills, with the Downfall impressively in view again ahead. It's a lovely narrow, level path, through heather and bilberries, which leads you along the hillside, with the morning sun sparkling on the reservoir when I was last here. Your path meets the path which has come up the valley from Hayfield (a quick way back if you have decided you need one). It continues along the hillside to display the Downfall closer at hand before you swing to the left.

Where the path forks, do not descend the eroded path on the right to the footbridge, but continue along the hillside. You can see your route climbing by the stream ahead. You descend gradually to the stream, ford it, and begin the climb up William Clough – or perhaps this is a good spot for a coffee-stop before you reach the exposed plateau-edge.

". . . Kinder Reservoir in its bowl of hills, with the Downfall impressively in view again ahead . . ."

The path takes you backwards and forwards through the stream, but you should be able to keep your feet dry. When there's a choice of sides, it doesn't matter whether the stream's to left or right, but always keep in the clough and don't go way up its side. If you are geomorphologically-inclined, you will note that the valley has excellent examples of interlocking spurs. Where the clough forks, the path takes the right-hand branch.

Just when you're wondering if the climb will end (there's precision for you!), it does, at the head of an eroded section of path, with two large cairns and a superb view back over the reservoir to Chinley Churn. Well, to be honest, there's just a little more uphill to the signpost at the junction with the Pennine Way, along which you turn right on the climb (er, sorry about that) to the edge of the Kinder plateau. If it seems a long way up to the cairn, Kirk Yetholm must seem an eternity away to the group of four young people I've just chatted to as they begin their journey to Scotland.

You can look back over Glossop and, yes, Winter Hill north of Bolton is just visible, while the Pennines lead northwards to Blackstone Edge, to give hope to the Pennine Wayfarers. As you stride along the broad path on the escarpment, you can appreciate the gritstone rocks beneath your feet and close at hand and the distant views of Peak District and Mersey plain.

Detailed instructions are not necessary; just enjoy yourself. As you round the corner above the rocks of Sandy Heys, the Mermaid's Pool is below and before you, and you keep along the edge towards the Downfall. In places you twist and turn between and across great slabs of millstone grit and then you reach Kinder Downfall. When I last did this walk, a strong wind from the north-west was blowing much of the River Kinder's flow back into the air. The sun was out and I spent some time scrambling over the rocks to take photographs. The fall and fountain were spectacular.

Cross the shallow river on the stone slabs above the waterfall, perhaps needing to keep well back from the edge to avoid wind-blown spray, and change direction to follow the plateau-edge again. Cairns lead you on to the crossing of Red Brook, also on gritstone slabs, beyond which you keep with the cairns along the upper path to continue along the edge of the plateau. There are unavoidable patches of peat, but they're nothing to what you have to endure on other stretches of the Pennine Way.

Be guided by the cairns, and the trig. point on Kinder Low will be to your left when you reach an impressive cairn. Here the path leaves the edge of the plateau to cut off the long ridge stretching out to Kinderlow End. Your path, no longer clear on the ground, bears a little left here, over a hummock with jagged rocks on its right-hand side, keeps to the right of the obvious pile of outcropping rocks ahead, Edale Rocks, and then descends through the grass to the path clearly seen ahead and marked by a cairn.

For the direct path back to Hayfield, turn right when you reach the cairn; for the optional diversion to the Wool Packs, turn left. Whichever you do, make sure you don't miss the view down Edale and over to Mam Tor.

On the diversion, keep to the path by the wall, with the Noe Stool prominent before you. The path curves round to the right past the Noe Stool and then climbs to the right of a group of rocks with Pym Chair to the left. Past those rocks you find an amazing landscape littered with the

Wool Packs, sculptured by wind, rain, sun and frost. They make me think of the giant heads on Easter Island. Go as far as you like among them. It's worth going down the path which leads off to the right for a close-up, and there is almost bound to be some shelter whichever way the wind is blowing. Ahead are Back Tor and Lose Hill on the far side of Edale, back to the right is Jacob's Ladder climbing up from Edale, and you can look out over the White Peak's limestone tops.

Now retrace your steps via Pym Chair and Noe Stool to the cairn. At the cairn, keep on if you've been to the Wool Packs or turn right if you haven't. The path makes its way, exceedingly rockily, along the hillside and below the crag of Swine's Back. Keep above the wall and do not turn down the broad path on the left towards Brown Knoll. Only when you reach the corner of the field, with its ruined sheepfold, do you turn down to the left beside the wall.

Climb the stile at the bottom of the field, and turn right through the gateway. There on your right is Edale Cross, a mediaeval cross where three of the wards of the Royal Forest of the Peak met on a packhorse track. Follow the track ahead downhill towards Hayfield and the plain, with a fine view of South Head to the left.

Descend the track to cross the stream at Stony Ford and then, a few yards farther on, climb the stile on the right and turn left along the path for Hayfield. The path is a very easy one and hardly climbs – that's good at this stage of a walk. It gives an excellent view of South Head and Dimpus Clough on the left and then Hayfield and Greater Manchester appear ahead.

Descend to the fork and take the path which bears left, not the thin path which turns left. Cross the ladder-stile over a wall that looks recently rebuilt (some task) and follow the path up and across the field, aiming for the buildings of Hayfield and round to the right to a stile. The path is clear as it proceeds across the field ahead. At the next stile, a sign points you onwards again, to a stile beside a gate, from where the path bears left. You come to a choice of stone step-stile or wooden stile on the left and, over either, descend the path towards Tunstead Clough Farm.

Through the kissing-gate, you leave the National Trust's Kinder Estate and descend to the farm drive. Turn along it to the right between the farm buildings, and keep on the drive as it crosses a stream and swings left. When you reach the road, walk along it beside the River Sett.

Where the road turns right over the bridge, you don't. You stay on the left bank of the river and follow the drive through the campsite. Beyond the amenity block (where you may be able to check whether the weather forecast was correct), a footpath continues along the riverbank. The path becomes a track, the track becomes a drive (note the creeper-crawling house across the river), and the drive becomes a quiet road leading into Hayfield.

Perhaps by now you are feeling you'd like to sit gnomishly in that pleasant garden with the three gnomes already ensconced there, but you've not far to go now. At the main road, turn right to the church, left before it, and through the subway or over the crossing back to the car park and bus station – but perhaps only after sampling a source of refreshment.

15. LAPWINGS AND LEGIONARIES

Uppermill – Greenfield – Bishop Park – Castleshaw – Uppermill.

Distance: $8^1/_2$ miles and $11^1/_2$ miles.

Starting points:

Saddleworth Museum car park, Uppermill; Pathfinder Map 713, Oldham, map reference 996055 (or Landranger Map 109, Manchester).

Greenfield railway station; Pathfinder Map 713, Oldham, map reference 992047 (or Landranger Map 109, Manchester).

How to get there:

By car – to the car park near Saddleworth Museum at Uppermill on the A670 between Ashton-under-Lyne and Huddersfield.

By train – to Greenfield on the Manchester to Huddersfield line.

This is a walk in a strange land, the land of Saddleworth. It's an area of scattered farms and groups of houses dispersed over hills and valley-sides with larger settlements in the bottoms of valleys, an area that has sought to maintain its independence and distinctiveness.

It no doubt did the same when Agricola arrived in the first century A.D. to establish a fort at Castleshaw. As the lapwings screamed their resentment at my alien presence in their territory, perhaps so did the Britons when the legionaries marched here. The fort was a day's march from Manchester, so a visit seems appropriate for this book.

The full walk is $11^1/_2$ miles long, starting from either Uppermill or Greenfield station and largely keeping to the hilltops except when there are valleys to be crossed. There are two shorter walks: a southern one which I call the Bishop circuit as it reaches its climax with the views from Bishop Park, and that returns via the upper valley of the Tame and a delightful stretch of the old Greenfield – Delph railway, a distance of $8^1/_2$ miles. The other shorter walk is of $9^1/_2$ miles from Uppermill or $10^1/_2$ miles from Greenfield, and begins along the old railway and the

Tame valley before reaching the Roman fort at Castleshaw, and I refer to
that as the Castleshaw circuit.

I think this is a fascinating area, and I hope the walks capture its spirit.

The Walk

From the car park at Saddleworth Museum, walk back along the road
towards Manchester and, at the bridge across the Huddersfield Narrow
Canal, descend the steps on the left to the canal towpath to walk
between the River Tame and the canal and past pretty gardens. At the
first bridge across the canal, before you reach the mills, turn right over
the waterway to the road, and up the steps and path opposite to reach
the next road. Turn left along by the railway as far as the bridge by
Greenfield station, where you turn right, over the line.

Those starting from the Huddersfield-bound platform of Greenfield
station cross the footbridge, turn left out of the station, and left across
the road-bridge, now with those who started from Uppermill.

At the far end of the bridge, turn right up the road towards Saddleworth
Golf Club. If you have started from Greenfield station to walk the
Castleshaw circuit, you continue along the road. Everyone else will leave
the road after only a few yards by climbing the stile on the left and
following the path which gains height above the road. To the right you
look down on Uppermill, up the Chew valley, and across to the war
memorial on Pots and Pans.

The path takes you up and along the hillside and you can look up to the
head of the Diggle valley, over Uppermill and Diggle to Millstone Edge
and Standedge and the roads climbing over the Pennines. Slowly you
leave the sound of road and rail below you. Then your way is blocked
by a quarry. You obey the "Danger – Keep Out" sign by turning up to
the left and following the quarry fence uphill. The quarrying operations
add interest of a sort and, beyond, you can see Harrop Edge on your
return route.

The television mast on the summit of Wharmton appears on the left, you
can see back to Dove Stone, the lowest of the Chew valley reservoirs,
and you arrive at the corner of the quarry fence. Here turn right and
make for the track leading towards the shed on the hillside, with the

Walk 15

A·B·C·D·E Castleshaw Circuit
E·D·C   Bishop Circuit

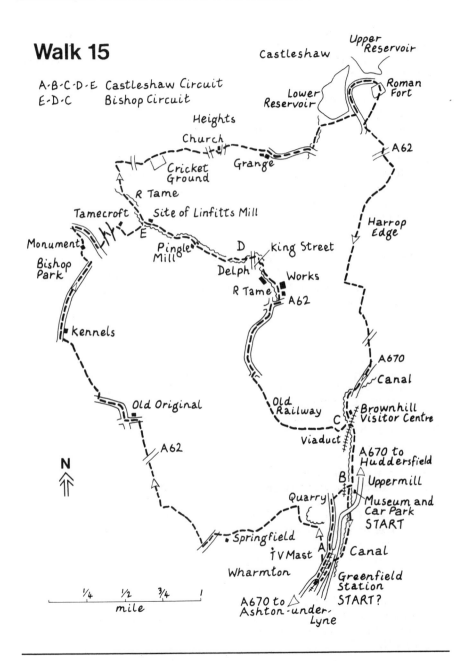

quarry and the cricket field down to your right. Don't go all the way to the shed but take the clear track up to the left; it's the continuation of Moorgate, the path you can see coming up from the right between quarry and golf-course.

Follow the track up over the skyline, with the mast still to your left and the great bowl of the Chew valley farther to your left. The gradient eases and, on my last visit, peewits were driven to distraction by my presence, and then came the unmistakable sound of a snipe drumming. To the right the Castleshaw reservoirs can be seen and then, over the crest of the hill, a totally different view greets you. From the junction with the track to the mast, you look out across Greater Manchester to the power station cooling-towers of the Mersey valley, to hilltop Oldham and its civic tower, and then Winter Hill. It's not a wild view, but it is of great interest.

Strictly speaking you should not bear right through the gateway and along the track but should be on the left-hand side of the wall ahead parallel to the track and aiming for Oldham. Either side of the wall, when you reach the next gateway bear left along the walled, grassy track with Grasscroft and Mossley, Stalybridge and the Peak District down the valley to your left, and a good view of your railway route to Greenfield.

Over the three-way stile, keep on along the walled track, past the entrance to Springfield Farm, to the road. At the road, turn left for impressive views of the Tame and Chew valleys and, at the first house on the right, Cartshead Nook, turn up the path through the garden. I know it doesn't look like a right of way, but it is. Keep to the right of the house and climb the stone path to the top of the garden and along the walled track beyond. This track can be boggy.

Go over the stile ahead and follow the right-hand wall, through a meadow of clover and ladysmock when I was last here, to the next gate. Squeeze past the gate and bear left towards the church. On the far side of the field, follow the wall to your right until you reach a stile just before a wall joins yours from the left. Climb the stile and keep on beside the right-hand wall (making for Oldham Civic Centre), keep to the right of the hollow of the pond, and turn right through the stile beside the gateway.

Now keep straight on beside the wall on the left, uphill towards the radio mast. The valley-heads at Castleshaw and Diggle are impressive to the right. Stiles lead you up to the A62, which you cross carefully, through the stile opposite and up by the left-hand wall to the next road, from where you can look back to much of your earlier route and again down the Tame valley to the Peak District.

Turn left along the road, past the row of stone cottages and the Old Original pub, to the crossroads. There turn right up Back Lane and left by the masts so as not to enter the quarry. Manchester is to your left and Winter Hill straight ahead.

Opposite the first house on the left, go through the stile beside the gate on the right-hand side of the road and up to the fence before what I assume is an old quarry and tip. Bear left beyond the fence and under the power-line. If you aim for the very red housing estate (I am referring to its physical colour, not the political proclivities of its inhabitants, which are unknown to me), you should come to a wooden stile, and over that you cross a track and go through the stile in the wall opposite.

Cross the field, the residence of two over-familiar horses when I was last here, to the corner of the wall ahead, where there is another stile. Go through that and keep by the right-hand wall. There are tremendous views over Greater Manchester, the Mersey plain and round to Winter Hill and the West Pennine moors, Knowle Hill to the north of Bury, and the hills round Whitworth north of Rochdale – too many to name even if I could identify them all.

Keep on over a succession of stiles, always having a wall on your right. By a gate, you reach a road, cross it, and go through the stile in the wall opposite, aiming a little to the right of the white house, to a gap-stile in the wall ahead. Through that, turn left alongside the wall. At the bottom of the field a footpath sign shows you the site of the stile onto the road.

Turn right up the road, past the kennels, and on uphill, with the monument at Bishop Park now very prominent. I contemplated going over the stile on the left after the next farm, but the huge handlebar horns of two highland cattle (sex indistinguishable owing to their position and hirsuteness!) deterred me.

I therefore continued to the stile on the crest of the road before turning left across the field to the next stile and then up to the right to the monument. First comes the trig. point, then the monument, smaller than it has been looking from a distance and commemorating the gift of the land of Bishop Park by William and Ann Bishop to the people of Oldham. Finally, there is what I assume to be a vandalised toposcope.

What can you see? There is the radio mast on Windy Hill, above the summit of the M62, with the valley of the infant Tame descending from it, to Delph down to the right. Then swing round across the views you've had earlier and over Heywood to the hills to the north. On a clear day it's a spot ripe for a coffee-break.

" . . . *with the monument at Bishop Park now very prominent* . . . "

You now have to cross the upper Tame valley and make for the church at Heights, just to the right of the nearest electricity pylon. So continue along the path to the car park and out to the road, along which you turn right past a farm with a catslide roof at the far end. Where the road forks, go over the stile on the left and descend to the left of the fence round the wood. Turn right for a few yards down the road and then back to the left down the drive for Tamecroft Farm.

At the first fork, bear right downhill and then, not far past the fork (where there were white goats in the trees), carefully climb the stile on the right and go down to the bottom right-hand corner of the field. Turn right to keep to the left of the shed but, above Tamecroft Farm, go through the gap in the fence ahead, and bear left to the stile. Descend the first set of steps ahead and turn right down the drive, which takes you between a house and a bungalow.

Between the bushes at the foot of the drive is a stile. You climb it and descend between the fence and the hawthorns. At its foot, the path is stone-surfaced and snakes down to a stile. Cross it and go down to the left to a footbridge over the River Tame. Those doing the Bishop circuit turn right on the far bank here at Linfitts, while those doing the full walk turn left, now in the company of those walking the Castleshaw circuit, who have come up the valley.

The full walkers and the Castleshaw circuiteers (who follow the route of the full walk from hereon) have an easy, level path up the valley and over a metal footbridge, across which two horses clanked noisily, to a stile beside a gate leading to another bridge. Cross stile and bridge in this pleasant spot and follow the track beside the wood and then uphill through it. Bluebells, rhododendrons and pink purslane were in massed bloom when I last walked along here.

At the fold with its attractive old houses, turn up the drive to the right, with another fine house along the hillside to the left. Beyond the castellated gateposts, go up the path on the far side of the road, past the end of the stone row, with Heights church on the skyline not far ahead.

Cross the road and walk up to the cricket ground. Keep along the left-hand side of the pitch – unless they're desperately short of players and you are roped in for the match before completing the walk – and through the stile in the wall ahead. The monument to the Bishops is now visible behind. In the next field there is no path visible on the ground; aim just a little to the left of the church to the stile at the right-hand side of a narrow field and, over the stile, ascend the narrow field (which soon widens out) towards the second-from-the-right of the four farms ahead.

Over the stile, keep by the left-hand wall. When you reach the road, turn left for a few paces and then over the stile on the right and up to Heights church, more properly St. Thomas Friarmere, built in 1765 as Delph's church but now succeeded by one in a location more convenient for its customers. A stile brings you to the road at the entrance to the churchyard and beside the Royal Oak. You can look out to Pots and Pans, the mast at Wharmton near your start, and the Bishop monument. Delph is down below.

Turn up the road between church and pub and then, at the end of the pub car park, go over the stile on the right and keep the wall on your right as you make your way along the hillside to the next stile. Over that, continue by the right-hand wall and, as you descend, you can look across to the left to see the Roman fort on the flat terrace above the lower reservoir at Castleshaw. The view may not be quite as dramatic as that looking down on Hardknott fort in the Lake District, but I think it's exciting nevertheless.

The next stile is in the bottom left-hand corner of the field and from there the path follows the fence above the sunken lane, not down on it. It's nearer to the farm that a stile lets you out onto the track, which you follow downhill. Keep to the left of the buildings of Grange, its name signifying its monastic origins, and then let the road take you down to the right and into the bottom of the valley.

Cross bridge or ford, climb the stile on the left, and keep by the stream. The fort is now above you and the sentries are marking your every step – as are the ewes and lambs. You cross to the far bank and then, just before the dam, back again, and climb the path outside the waterworks wall, over the ladder-stile in the wall, and up the steps to the track round the lower reservoir.

Follow the track to the right to the end of the dam and then bear left through the wall to the road in front of the house. Turn left along the road for views across the reservoir in its bowl of hills and then keep on the road as it bends round to the right, gently uphill to the upper reservoir.

Do not cross that dam but continue to ascend to the right for a few more yards before turning back through the gate on the right. Then go through the gap in the fence on the left to the fort. The rough field leads to obvious ramparts and ditch and an interpretation board for the later fortlet, which helps greatly. But I still think the most impressive view was from Heights.

Go diagonally across the site, aiming south, and you will reach an interpretation board for the fort and its context. You will see that your route along the footpath beyond the fort is going to lead you across the line of the Roman road over the Pennines from Manchester. Curlew called and larks sang as I sat eating my lunch and pondering that no Roman soldier could have eaten a delicious shepherd's pie like mine – because he wouldn't have had any potatoes.

Look up to the rugged rocks of Millstone Edge behind you and then leave the fort by the southern corner, near the "Welcome to Castleshaw" interpretation board. Go through the gap in the fence beyond the "little and large" stones. Bear left down the field towards where the road crosses the valley and a footpath sign will come into view in the corner of the field.

Through the wicket-gate, turn left along the road but, where the road turns right, you bear left through the gate and up the fenced and walled green track, wet in its lower reaches. The sunken track bends right to join a farm drive and arrives at the A62. You can look down on the fort before crossing the road and ascending the walled track almost opposite, near the Saddleworth Hotel.

At the crossroads of tracks, turn right along Harrop Edge, but keep looking back at the sun-filled bowl of Castleshaw. Well, it was when I was last there! As the track rises, you can look back left to spoilheaps from the Standedge tunnels, while much of your earlier route can be seen to the right. The track bends right and then left and then pursues a straight course aiming for the mast on Wharmton. Pots and Pans is – or are – in view again to the left, and to the right roads descend tortuously into Delph.

The track descends very gently and then levels off, with a long field on the left. At the end of the field, go through the stile or gate on the left (before the end of the high stone wall and opposite a stile on the other side of the track) and keep by the wall on the right to cross the ridge. Over the step-stile, continue by the wall for a super view over Diggle and up to the head of its valley, and then down the line of the canal and railway towards Manchester.

Turn right along the path you meet, an airy hillside path, and through a
stile to a junction of walled tracks. Turn left down the track towards the
pallet-works and keep on it as it turns right to descend the hillside,
echoing the path near the start of the walk. The path crosses a road and
goes through the stile opposite, to keep to the right of the hedge.
Negotiate nettles, climb an impressive "staircase stile", and you are soon
down on the A670.

Turn right along the road past the Navigation Inn, which correctly hints
at the proximity of the canal. Not much farther on, cross the canal and
turn right down onto the towpath. On the far bank is the trans-shipment
shed, used for the storage of goods being transferred from canal to road
before the completion of the canal tunnel through Standedge.

Beyond a low road bridge over the canal, the Saddleworth railway
viaduct strides across the Tame valley (you need to mind your head on
the former but not on the latter). Between the two is the Brownhill
Visitor Centre with toilets and a good range of publications. Continue
under the viaduct, now joined by those who have walked the Bishop
circuit, and along the towpath in the viaduct's shadow, with the war
memorial prominent to the left.

An attractive, well-surfaced stretch of towpath takes you into Uppermill,
where you can cross the Tame by stepping-stones into a park or even
have a narrowboat trip. Cross the canal at the bridge to find the towpath
again opposite the museum. If your walk is to end in Uppermill, turn
back to the car park; if you are bound for Greenfield station, turn back to
the start of the walk and follow the instructions from there.

The Bishop Circuit

To complete the Bishop Circuit from Linfitts, turn right along the far
bank of the Tame, through the stones of the ruined Linfitts Mill, good
sites for seats for a picnic. It was a real sun-trap among the white of the
hawthorns when I last sat here.

Climb the path to the drive, turn right, and keep to the right of the old
cars and the old house. On the narrow path beyond, descend to the
footbridge and turn left along the far bank of the river. Climb the stile,
pass between the buildings of Pingle Mill, and take the road from the
mill. Where that turns left over the bridge, keep on along the track ahead
and then the path which continues through the stile.

" . . . along the towpath in the viaduct's shadow . . . " – Saddleworth

At the entrance to the children's playground, cross the stone bridge on the left and turn right, past the allotments, to recross the river and arrive at the stone bridge carrying Delph's main street, King Street, over the Tame. After any exploration of Delph, cross King Street and go along the path on the right bank of the river and, opposite the bridge on the right, cross the bridge on the left.

On the far bank, take the lower path, to the right, and, beyond the row of cottages, keep along by the river. Pass the works to right and left and then go through the archway in the buildings ahead and out to the road.

Turn right to the crossroads and then left along the road towards Uppermill, with the old Delph railway station on the right. Now there's a boring bit along the road, though it's improved by glimpses of the Tame. Help is at hand: after the weir on the river and opposite the former entrance to a mill, turn right up the unsigned road with a stone house on its left. At the T-junction, bear left through the stile and turn left along the old railway line for an exceedingly pleasant mile.

You go through two short tunnels and over a bridge, with Dobcross to your left. There are birds and trees and flowers in plenty. A straight stretch leads you to a gate and stiles with a fence across the track ahead, and here you must turn right and then down the road to the left under the line. Brownhill Visitor Centre is across the valley to your left and Saddleworth viaduct is impressive before you.

Cross the canal beneath the viaduct and, perhaps after a diversion left to the Visitor Centre, turn right along the towpath, now with those who've done the full walk or the Castleshaw circuit.

The Castleshaw Circuit

If you start from Greenfield station, turn left out of the station, left over the bridge, and right along the road towards Saddleworth Golf Club. Continue along the road, not bearing right to Top o'th Croft Cottage, with the war memorial on Pots and Pans up to your right and Uppermill, down in the valley ahead. Beyond Ladcastle Farm, bear right down the track with a wall on the right, the old route of Moorgate, and, at the fork, bear right downhill. Cross the railway cautiously on the level-crossing and turn right, downhill still, over the canal, and left along the towpath.

If you start from the car park in Uppermill, walk back along the road towards Manchester and, at the bridge across the canal, turn back right along the towpath. At the next bridge, recross the canal and turn left along the towpath.

All now walk along a stretch of canal which in summer is beautifully green. As you approach Dungebooth Lock, Saddleworth viaduct appears ahead and dominates the view. Under the viaduct, turn left over the bridge, which enables you to see just how narrow the locks are. Having crossed the bridge, ascend the lane, go through the arch under the old railway, and turn right up to the line and left along it.

The line is well-surfaced, very pleasant, and furnished with benches. To your right is Dobcross. Two horses thundered past; were they descendents of the "Delph Donkey", the horse which originally hauled trains along here and gave its name to the line? You cross a bridge and then – great excitement! – go through two tunnels, or at least wide bridges. There were masses of bluebells and pink purslane, and the many birds included a wagtail.

Unfortunately, before a high bridge over the line, you have to leave the track through the stile by the gate on the right, signposted to Delph and Denshaw. Turn left, and then go down to the right to the road, where you turn left. Keep along the road beside the River Tame, rather an anti-climax after the pleasures of the line. You can see its old goods shed on the left, then the old station and even some rolling-stock.

At the road junction by the weavers' houses of four storeys, turn right along the A62 and then turn left through the archway before the Old Bell Inn. Keep along the roadway past the factory and then beside the river for an interesting industrial interlude. Do not cross the first footbridge but keep to the right of the row of houses across your path. Cross the next footbridge, but only as far as the path, and then turn right between river and leat.

The interesting buildings of Delph may tempt you off the route to explore, but wait a minute or two more. Along the path to the right, where the leat comes through the wall, note that the stone slab is "A Private Road".

At the public road, by the Rose and Crown, your route goes straight across to continue beside the river, but you may want to turn left to see Delph. Back between the Tame and the Rose and Crown, go through the stile ahead and over the next footbridge, to have the river on your left. The monument in Bishop Park is on the hill ahead, to the left of the farm on the skyline.

At the stone bridge, cross the river into Swan Meadow, turn right and, through the stile beside the gate, follow the track along the valley floor. Keep on along the road ahead and between the buildings of Pingle Mill, the path being just to the right of the old stone buildings. You leave the mill buildings over a stile to find a field path leading up the valley still to a footbridge, which you cross, to continue upstream on the far bank. It is uphill, as well.

You pass an old stone house, with a fascinating collection of old cars, and then bear left down a path off the drive. It takes you through the remains of the buildings of Linfitts Mill, with massive blocks of stone, to another footbridge. You keep on up the valley, together with those doing the full walk.

16. TUNNELS AND TURNPIKES

Marsden – Tunnel End – Diggle Edge – Diggle – Millstone Edge – Close
Gate Bridge – Marsden.

Distance: between 5 miles and $11^1/_2$ miles.

Starting Points:

Marsden railway station; Pathfinder Map 702, Huddersfield and
Marsden, map reference 047118 (or Landranger Map 110, Sheffield and
Huddersfield).

Tunnel End Canal and Countryside Centre, Marsden; Pathfinder Map
702, Huddersfield and Marsden, map reference 040119 (or Landranger
Map 110, Sheffield and Huddersfield).

Diggle Fields car park, Diggle; Pathfinder Map 714, Holmfirth and
Saddleworth Moor, map reference 006080 (or Landranger Map 110,
Sheffield and Huddersfield).

(You need both Pathfinder maps for all the walks except the shorter
Marsden circuit, for which the Huddersfield and Marsden map is
sufficient.)

How to get there:

By car – for Tunnel End Canal and Countryside Centre, make for
Marsden on the A62 between Oldham and Huddersfield. As the A62
descends towards Marsden after crossing Standedge, it bends round
right. At the 40 m.p.h. restriction sign, turn back sharp left downhill and
round to the right. At the junction among houses, turn back right to the
car park at Tunnel End.

– for Diggle Fields, bear right into Diggle off the A670 about a mile north
of Uppermill (in the direction of Marsden) and, after about another $3/_4$
mile, just past a mill on the right, turn right along Sam Road. At the first
bend, turn right into Diggle Fields car park.

By train – to Marsden on the Manchester to Huddersfield line.

By bus – from Manchester or Oldham to Tunnel End at Marsden (alight
at the 40 m.p.h. restriction sign on the descent into Marsden). Note that

the service is hourly on Saturday when it starts from Manchester and 2-hourly on Monday – Friday when it starts from Oldham.

– from Manchester to Oldham and then from Oldham to Diggle (alight at Diggle Fields car park in Sam Road).

– to reach Marsden from Diggle, follow the route of the walk to Harrop Green and then keep straight on, down and then steeply up Carr Lane to the A670, but note that the service between Diggle and Marsden is 2-hourly on Monday – Friday.

– to reach Diggle from Marsden, alight at Carr Lane, the first road on the left after the junction on the A62 and A670, walk steeply down Carr Lane and up to Harrop Green, but note that the service between Marsden and Diggle is 2-hourly on Monday – Friday.

The first time I walked this way, over Standedge, I much enjoyed the peace of the moorland tops and the views down into the Colne and Tame valleys. I could interpret a little of the industrial archaeological evidence scattered plentifully across the landscape. But then I discovered the Standedge Trail!

Much of the route of this walk coincides with the Standedge Trail and, for a full appreciation of this walk, I urge you to obtain a copy of the leaflet and map describing the Trail. You can buy it from the Tunnel End Canal and Countryside Centre and from information centres on the Greater Manchester side of Standedge too. It explains the fascinating series of routes successively crossing the Pennines here (this walk takes advantage of some of them) and the remains of the tunneling battles of canal and railway. Parts of your route follow old turnpikes and the paths of the canal horses as they came over the top while the narrowboats were legged through far below.

The full circular route from Marsden station to Diggle and back to Marsden is about $11^1/_2$ miles. You could walk a shorter circuit from Marsden up onto the top and back to Marsden ($5^1/_2$ miles), or a matching circuit from Diggle (6 miles), or a circuit of 8 miles from Marsden to include all the tops but avoiding the descent to and climb from Diggle. Or, you could do a linear walk from Marsden to Diggle (5 miles) or from Diggle to Marsden ($6^1/_2$ miles). But note that, except on Saturdays, the bus between Diggle and Marsden is of less than hourly frequency. It runs along the A670 at Diggle and not on the route of the walk there, although later the walk does cross the bus route on the A62 in several places.

So there you are: follow in the footsteps of those who built and used the roads, canals and railways across the Pennines, and experience marvellous scenery as well.

THE WALK

From the Huddersfield-bound platform of Marsden station, climb the steps to the road and turn left over the bridge and across the line and the Huddersfield Narrow Canal. Follow the road round to the left to the Railway Inn and then turn back left along the canal towpath, with its information board. You're making for Tunnel End.

The pleasant stretch of canal, with bluebells and broom and heather, takes you darkly under the railway to a canal warehouse, with a stream cascading down steps between the railway tunnel entrances to your left. Now cross the bridge over the canal and, on the far bank, turn left to the information centre at Tunnel End Cottages, good for views of trains.

Return towards the bridge and then turn back left up the footpath beside the information boards and up the steps. It is up this path that those arriving by car begin the walk. Go through the stile in the wall on the right and turn left up the road over the outfall from Tunnel End Reservoir. Follow the road round to the left and up to the A62 which provides a panoramic view of Tunnel End and the curves of the railway line; it's a pity steam trains are so few. This is the view with which the bus-travellers will begin their walk.

Turn left along the main road with Marsden in the valley before you and turn right up the walled path at the far end of the row of stone houses on the right. The path climbs beside the left-hand wall and then, when the wall ends, you go over the stile on the left and along the hillside towards Old Mount Road.

As you approach the stream, keep to the right of the wall, climb the stile on the left, and ascend by the left-hand wall, towards the chimneys. When you reach the old farmhouse, turn right up the sunken track, old with walls and bleached sheep-skulls. Soon Butterley Reservoir comes

Walk 16

1/4 1/2 3/4 1
mile

Close Gate Bridge

Tunnel End START?

Station START

Dark Lane

Owlers

Marsden A62 to Hudders-field

Farm

Pule Hill

A62

Dinner Stone

Millstone Edge

Thieves Clough

B

A

Standedge Cutting

Redbrook Resr.

Mount Bar

A62 to Oldham

Brun Clough Reservoir

Bus Stop

Carr Lane

Ridge Lane

Diggle Edge

Boat Lane

A670 to Uppermill

HG

Hotel

Diggle

Mill

Diggle Fields Car Park START?

To A670 and Uppermill

N

A·B Shorter Marsden Circuit
B·A Shorter Diggle Circuit
C·D 8·mile Marsden Circuit

HG Harrop Green

into view ahead to the left with high Pennine hills beyond. Trains are now far below and rocky outcrops are at hand.

" . . . *a panoramic view of Tunnel End and the curves of the railway line* . . . "

Over the gate across the track, your route continues uphill beside the wall on the left. The track levels off, joins a better track, and keeps on ahead along it, with Butterley Reservoir spread out to the left and bleak hills ahead. Sheep stood and stared in windswept fleeces and a ram sneezed and sneezed with snuff-like vigour.

Your track is level as you've done the real climbing for the first part of the walk, while the roads from Marsden struggle up from the left. You meet Old Mount Road and turn right along it to its junction with Mount Road at Mount Bar. These were successive turnpike routes.

Those returning to Marsden by the short circuit turn right along the road. All others go down the path on the far side of the road, cross the bridge over the stream flowing on slabs of rock and bear left to the footpath sign. After I had crossed the bridge, a ewe and two lambs sedately used it and climbed the path to the road.

At the sign, turn right and follow the path between the two gullies across a land of wind, larks and curlew – and were those the calls of golden plover in the breeze? The path takes you to a waymark post, where you turn left and you can see that you're going to have a very gentle ascent – the continuation of the turnpike routes. This length of old turnpike, following the easiest gradient, through nodding plumes of cotton grass, is my favourite stretch of the whole walk, most atmospheric. I find it difficult not to click my tongue and whinny. Pule Hill, to be visited on your return, is to the right.

You cross a channel linking the moor-top reservoirs (to provide water for the canal) and there is a fine view back along the turnpike's route. It's quite a surprise a few minutes later to look to the right and see a pub across Redbrook Reservoir with its boats. Stride across the stream flowing from the pool on the left and keep on the old road as it bears right uphill. As you approach another breach in the causeway of the road, turn right to cross the gully by a bouncy bridge and then back onto the original course. Pule Hill looks impressive behind.

The path leads on to the spoilheaps above the main road's Standedge Cutting, and you turn left alongside the fence. Then a great view down the Tame valley and over Greater Manchester is revealed, with the Pennine Way and Millstone Edge to your right. You descend to a car park and there cross the Pennine Way.

For the 8-mile route back to Marsden, cross the road here. But for Diggle keep on down the road past Brun Clough Reservoir and then, where the fence rejoins the road, turn left up the bank and go through the wicket-gate on the right. You can look down on a tunnel spoilheap and along the railway line towards Manchester. Bear left downhill and over the little stone bridge to the drive. Follow it downhill past the house, with tunnel shafts on the right.

Beyond the house, follow the wall and spoilheap round to the right; here is industrial archaeology with a vengeance! Cross a gully and keep beside the wall as you descend gently towards railway, canal and Diggle. The path brings you down to a gate at Diggle Edge Farm and you continue downhill following the Oldham Way (you'll have seen its owl waymarks earlier) to the right of the house. Descend winding Boat Lane, the canal horses' route, with the mast above Greenfield ahead of you.

The lane takes you down to the Diggle Hotel and the road, but I suggest that, before you reach the hotel, you turn back to the right along the track which crosses the mouths of the railway tunnel. That way you won't go past the door of the pub! It serves food and drink, which may be welcome at this stage, so you may well wish to visit it and then turn right along the road bridge beyond it.

At the end of either bridge, turn left, continue to the telephone box, and then turn sharp right back up Harrop Green Lane. (Near the telephone box is a bus stop for Oldham and bus passengers from Oldham should alight here to start the walk. Here also is Diggle Fields car park, through which you can reach the mouth of the canal tunnel, and it is from this car park that some may begin the walk.)

At the treed green in the middle of Harrop Green, a delightful grouping of houses, turn right up walled Ridge Lane. Note the watershot masonry of the farm on the left. The narrow road climbs gently between hawthorns back to the hills, and the spoilheap of your earlier route is plain to the right. Millstone Edge is on the skyline ahead of you and there are fine views back down the Tame valley. The sound of Yorkshire-bound trains is suddenly extinguished as they enter the tunnel.

After the interesting houses with long lines of windows, you reach a more main road at the Old Toll House, typically at a junction to catch travellers on both roads. Here you bear right uphill past an informative milestone. Where the road bears right before the handsome, white house, leave the road for the signposted track on the left towards the fine buildings of Dean Head. Follow the drive round to the left over the stream, go through the gate on the right, and ascend the field and steep bank to the stile on the skyline to the left of the large shed. You emerge in a stoneyard with window-tracery and turn left to the road.

Turn right along the A62 and, before crossing the ravine, go through the stile on the left and up the field towards the pair of farmhouses. Keep to the left of the ruined wall. I met a rapid rabbit and a haughty pair of much-goslinged geese. As you near the houses, descend to the stile in the fence on the right and turn left along the edge of the garden of the restored house.

Now turn right along the road but, when it turns right, turn left up the farm drive, round the bend to the left, and then, before the farm entrance, go up the signposted footpath on the right. Here the owner of a hang-glider was wondering if the wind was too strong for flying. It was great for walking.

The path takes you, between rocky outcrops, up onto Millstone Edge and the Pennine Way, from where I could look down onto Castleshaw Reservoirs, across to Winter Hill near Bolton, and down the Tame valley over Greater Manchester to the Peak District.

If you turn left along the path and over the stile, a few minutes' exhilarating walk (yes, the wind was too strong for hang-gliding) will bring you to a trig. point from where I could see out over the Mersey plain to the left of Winter Hill, way into Yorkshire to the north-east, and to Holme Moss television mast to the south-east. To the north-west I thought I could see Darwen Tower.

Farther along the path is the distinctive rock of the Dinner Stone and before that is a large cairn with, on the rock below, memorial plaques to Ammon Wrigley, poet of Saddleworth, and others. It's a fine spot and the day echoed Ammon Wrigley's words about being "flung to the winds in my hill country".

Now return to the stile and the top of the path by which you reached the Edge and continue along the Edge, over a stile, through the wall on the left, and over another stile to a post. To the right you have a last look down the Tame valley as you turn left towards Marsden (now with those doing the 8-mile circuit), aiming for Pule Hill and not up to the wall on the left. Pass a National Trust sign for Close Moss and keep on ahead. The incline on the side of Pule Hill is obvious.

The path swings right to cross the well-made bridge over Thieves Clough. Probably constructed by Blind Jack Metcalfe of Knaresborough, it provides shelter if needed on a bleak day. When you reach the wall and LNWR boundary stone, with shaft and spoilheaps beyond, bear right, over the stream, and follow the path round to the road.

Cross a substantial slab of stone, read about the Standedge Trail, and turn left along the road. Marvel at the amount of material excavated by primitive means and then take the road on the right. The colour of the water emerging from Redbrook Reservoir suggests it's well-named.

Continue along the road until you reach a sign to Boat Lane on the right, by a footbridge, just before you reach the dying end of Pule Hill. You, however, turn left along the path on the opposite side of the road (unless you're doing the shorter Diggle circuit, in which case you continue along the road). Contour around Pule Hill above the A62, with the super bowl of Haigh Clough ahead. It's a strange mixture of man and nature here: wind, sun, clouds, hills and the grim rocks of millstone grit, and then the ruins of buildings, shafts, incline and spoilheaps. They didn't seem to worry about these things in the last century; how much better are we?

At the track beyond the incline, do not go up to the right but maintain your level along the hillside (there's some sign of a path) and then follow the clearer path round the foot of the spoilheap and along the hillside again. At the fork, keep to the lower path as there's no point in climbing, and the path leads you to a sturdy wooden stile in a stone wall beside a National Trust sign. Continue along the hillside and over three wooden bridges to white-painted Owler's Farm. There turn left through the wrought-iron gates and down the drive to the road. When I was last here, the footpath signs seemed to have turned themselves round.

Turn right down the road, past the house called Shepherds Boy. Just beyond it, the road bends right but you turn left down Dark Lane, a lovely, grassy, walled path. It steepens in its lower reaches and is a real gem of a path with views to the hills beyond. It ends at the pretty stream of Red Brook, turning the stones here red too. There is a ford but it's probably drier to cross the rocks at the foot of the path. It appears there was once a bridge here, but not when I've come this way.

Turn right along the track, over the lovely little packhorse bridge of Close Gate Bridge, which carried the mediaeval track of Rapes Highway, and along the stream-bank path shaded by beech trees. When you reach the road and discover you have been near Willykay Clough, keep along the road, downhill and still alongside the stream. Pass an intriguing row of arched cottages at Lower Hey Green and the site of Tunnel End Reservoir, with Holme Moor dominating the view ahead – and no sign yet of railway or canal. The reservoir is but a shadow – or should it be reflection? – of its former self.

At the road junction by the Junction Inn, those wanting a bus back to Diggle, Oldham or Manchester should turn right up the road to the A62. All others should merely bear right down to Tunnel End Cottages. To walk back to Diggle, if you started from there, go up the path by the information boards. For Marsden station, cross the canal and turn left along the towpath until you get there.

Make sure you're on platform 2 when the Manchester train comes in, or you'll have a most unseemly dash over the bridge to catch it.

" . . . the lovely little packhorse bridge of Close Gate Bridge . . . "

Mount Bar to Pule Hill

To walk the shorter Marsden circuit, at Mount Bar turn right along the road and, after it has climbed a little over the end of Pule Hill, take the path on the right opposite the little footbridge and contour round the foot of Pule Hill.

Pule Hill to Mount Bar

For the shorter Diggle circuit, continue along the road past the end of Pule Hill to the road's junction with Old Mount Road at Mount Bar and turn down the path on the right to cross the stream.

Brun Clough Reservoir to Millstone Edge

For the 8-mile circuit from Marsden, from the car park before Brun

Clough Reservoir cross the road and go up the track with its Pennine Way signpost. Where the track forks, keep left to enter a cutting. Before the end of the cutting, turn right to follow the sign for the Oldham and Pennine Ways. The path takes you over slabs of millstone grit and up towards Millstone Edge. You will arrive at a cross-wall with a wooden stile in it. Do not cross it (unless you wish to make the diversion to the Dinner Stone, in which case keep straight on), but turn right to bear away from the cross-wall, now with those walking the main route.